CW00967678

GD Ma
How to Excel
Group Discussions

GYAN SHANKAR

1

Content

Chapter 1. What & Why GD? 4

Chapter 1
What & Why GD?

The importance of GD has increased in recent times due to its increasing role as an effective tool in problem-solving and decision-making. The best option is chosen by the group. While making a decision, the matter is discussed, analyzed, interpreted and evaluated.

Whether one is a student, a professional, or a company executive, effective GD skills are required. Students need to participate in academic discussions, meetings, and classroom sessions. Professionals have to participate in different meetings at the workplace. In all these situations, the ability to make a significant contribution to group deliberation and help the group make decisions is required.

Group Discussion or GD is a methodology used by an organization (Bank, Company, Institute, Business School etc.) to measure the required personality traits or skills that it desires in its members. It includes a candidate's in-depth knowledge of the topic, self-confidence, attitude, presence of mind in crisis, etiquette, team spirit etc. Nowadays GD is being extensively used along with personal interviews for the final selection of the candidate. GD is considerably different from public speaking, a general debate and an interview.

Usually, the institutes or companies conducting the GD know exactly what they want in their candidates. They are very clear about the specific traits that they want in their candidates. The Group Discussion helps them to analyze and mark the person having certain required traits, personality and skills that they desire in them. The reason why organizations and institutes put you through a Group discussion after testing your technical and conceptual skills in an examination is to get to know you as a person and gauge how well you will fit in their institute or organization.

It assesses the participant's behavioural traits, leadership skills, social skills, team skills, problem-solving skills and presence of mind. These also include reasoning ability, Inspiring ability, flexibility, creativity, out-of-the-box thinking, listening and articulation skills, situational handling ability, interpersonal ability to function as a team player, body language and attitude. These are the skills which are very much required to become a successful professional.

If we analyse the two words Group and Discussion. Group means several individuals who may or may not have interacted before. Discussion means exchanging information on a certain topic and coming (or not coming) to a concrete conclusion.

A discussion group is a group of individuals with similar interests who gather either formally or informally to discuss ideas, solve problems, or give comments. The major approaches are in person, via conference call, or website.

Group discussion is a systematic and purposeful oral process of formal exchange of views on a particular topic, issue, problem, or situation, which develops information and understanding essential for decision-making or problem-solving.

Here the exchange of ideas, thoughts and feelings takes place through oral communication. The exchange of ideas takes place in a systematic and structured way. Group Discussion is an invigorating discussion where a topic is analyzed and discussed, and in the end, the members are expected to come to a fair conclusion. It involves teamwork, but at the same time, it portrays individual personalities and skills.

Group discussion is an important tool for the assessment of a candidate's personality, subject knowledge, attitude, behaviour towards other team members, patience, self-confidence and the way a candidate presents his/her arguments.

Following are the *objectives* of the group discussion.

Quality of Leadership: To assess the leadership qualities of candidates. Observers note the people who are able to take the initiative in a group discussion and are able to convince others with the help of arguments.

In-depth Knowledge of the Subject: The observers, watch the candidate's knowledge about a particular topic or subject. It is also observed how coherently and emphatically a candidate expresses his views.

Analytical Abilities: Examiners observe the presence of analytical skills in candidates.

Language Proficiency and Communication Skills: Assess the candidate's command over language and how well he can communicate his perspective argument or opinion.

Self-Confidence: The candidate's self-confidence is also judged by the examiner/observer. Lacking in confidence decreases your chances of selection.

Problem-Solving and Decision-Making: Examiners aim to find out such candidates who are proficient in decision-making and can find a solution to a problem.

Behaviour with Other Team Members It is an essential quality which is observed during group discussion. How does a candidate behave with group members?

G D is essentially an interactive oral process. It involves a lot of group dynamics, that is, it involves both person-to-person as well as group-to-group interactions. Each of the participants has a platform and an opportunity to express his or her views and comments on the views expressed by other members of the group. Discussions of any sort are supposed to help us develop a better perspective on issues by bringing out diverse viewpoints. Whenever we exchange differing views on an issue, we get a clearer picture of the problem and can understand it. The understanding makes us better equipped to deal with the problem. This is precisely the main purpose of a discussion.

For any Group Discussion to be successful, the following characteristics are necessary:

Having a clear objective: An effective GD typically begins with a purpose stated by the initiator.

Motivated Interaction: When there is a good level of motivation among the members, they learn to subordinate their interests to the group interest and the discussions are more fruitful.

Logical Presentation: If the mode of interaction is not logical, few of the members in the group may dominate the discussion and thus will make the entire process meaningless.

Cordial Atmosphere: Development of a cooperative, friendly, cordial atmosphere and avoiding confrontation between the group members.

Effective Communication Skills: The success of a GD depends on the effective use of communication techniques. Like any other oral communication, clear pronunciation, simple language, and right pitch are the prerequisites of a GD. Non-verbal communication has to be paid attention to since means like body language convey a lot in any communication.

Participation by all candidates: When all the members participate, the GD becomes effective. Members need to encourage each other in the GD.

Chapter-2

Methodology of GD

Group Discussion, is held in small groups of candidates. It's a team game which can be nicely explained with an example, in a football game, where you play like a team, passing the ball to each team member and aim for a common goal. GD is also based on teamwork, incorporating the views of different team members to reach a common goal or output of the discussion.

Group Discussion is held, normally; for a limited period, 20-30 or 30-45 minutes, however; the duration of discussion is at the discretion of the panel that sets the time limit. However, the GD may be stopped earlier in certain exceptional circumstances. To warn the participants that discussion time is going to finish, a warning bell may be rung one minute before. Sometimes, evaluators may ask candidates to present a summary of the GD at the end. For topic-based GDs, 2 to 5 minutes of preparation time is given before the discussion time starts. For case studies, a longer time (up to 15 minutes) may be given. The normal discussion time is kept at 20 to 25 minutes.

Normally 8 to 10 participants are asked to sit together in a rectangular or circular arrangement for a group discussion. They may either have pre-determined seats or free seating may be allowed. The evaluators or examiners may be one or two experienced experts who sit separate from the participants but are in a position to observe all details.

In this methodology, the group of candidates is given a topic or a situation and then asked to think and discuss the topic. They are asked to discuss for a specific duration which may vary from one organization to another. The topic can be general or specific. Example: "Global Warming" or just a phrase saying "Where there's a will there's a way".

After announcing the topic, the total GD time, and explaining the general guidelines and procedures governing the GD, the panel withdraws to the background leaving the group completely free to carry on with the discussion on its own without any outside interference. The panel does not interfere during the discussion, it only observes. The panel at its discretion may provide some time to think over the topic or may ask them to start immediately. Soon after that, the topic or case to be discussed is given to the group members.

In the absence of a designated leader to initiate the proceedings of the discussion, the group is likely to waste time in cross-talks, low-key conversations, cross-consultations, asides, and so on. The confusion may last until someone in the group takes an assertive position and restores the chaos into order. It could be any candidate. The discussion carries on till the panel signals termination.

Process of Group Discussion can be divided into three stages, which are as follows:

Initiation of the GD

Body of the GD

Summarisation of the GD

Initiation of the GD

Any person in the group takes the lead and imitates the discussion.

Body of the GD

Every candidate gets an opportunity to present his views on the topic during this process. The expert assesses every candidate's contribution so everyone has to be positive. The observers also try to assess points and ideas raised by the participants. They will also assess the number of points raised, the relevance of the points and the creativity and uniqueness of the points.

All candidates try to present the important points and opinions during this time. The panel observes meticulously who takes the lead, who has deep knowledge, who encourages others, and who has the leadership qualities and team spirit. They may also observe whether the points by the candidates are directed to the entire group or to some particular participants and also who responds to the spoken points.

Summarisation of the GD

The summary must incorporate all the important points that came out during the discussion. About one minute before the end of the scheduled time, one of the evaluators rings a bell and asks the participants to sum up the discussion. If the participants have successfully concluded, one of them summarises the discussion and a conclusion is drawn. In some cases, the evaluators may ask each of the participants to sum up the discussion, by turns. Do not add anything once the GD has been summarised. The evaluators signal the end of the discussion, thank the participants and request them to leave the room.

At this time, the evaluators observe the reactions of the participants, who are low-spirited, upbeat or confident, who maintain their poise, does any participant ask any queries and if so, is the query relevant?

Most GDs do not have conclusions. A conclusion is where the whole group decides in favour or against the topic, as in a debate. But every GD requires to be summarised. You can summarise what the group has discussed in the GD in a nutshell, provided you are confident about doing so.

Keep the following points in mind while summarising a discussion

Avoid raising new points.

Avoid stating only your viewpoint or emphasising it.

Avoid dwelling only on one aspect of the GD.

Keep the summary brief and concise.

Chapter 3

Doubts Relating to GD Clarified.

Q. What is the normal duration of a GD?

Ans It is generally of 20-35- or 30-45-minute duration.

Q. Why panel does not appoint a Group Leader or Group Chairman?

Ans. The concept of GD is based on the belief that people working in a group cannot effectively work for results without a leader. The concept further believes that if no one is formally appointed a leader, the group will soon be following the viewpoint of one particular person in the group and that particular person will automatically emerge as a leader. The emerging leader will be the person who has some in-built talent different from others.

Q. How many panel members are there to evaluate?

Ans. There are usually 3-4 panel members to evaluate.

Q. Is their time given for preparation after the topic is given and before starting the GD?

Ans. Usually sometime (2-5 minutes) is given to collect one's thoughts, but there could be instances when this does not happen,

So, it is best not to bank on this.

Q. Should I address the panel or the group members?

Ans. doesn't ever make the mistake of addressing the panel members. The GD is between you and the other members, not the panel members. You must avoid even looking at the panel members while the GD is in progress. Just ignore their existence.

Q. What is the Group Size and seating arrangement like?

Ans. Generally, Group Size varies between 8-10 persons or sometimes more. Sitting arrangement, normally; it could be semi-circular, circular, or seated alongside a rectangular table. It is best not to bother about trivial issues like this, which you have no control over.

Q. Is there any particular seating arrangement, which is favourable to the participants?

Ans. If participants are asked to sit in a circle or a semi-circle, one position is as good as another but if you are asked to sit on either side of a rectangular table then choose a position as close to the center as possible.

Q. Who monitors the Group Discussion?

Ans. An Officer, usually known as an evaluator or Group Testing Officer (GTO), monitors the discussion.

Q. Who selects the topic of the Group Discussion?

In case, only one topic is given, there is no option than start a discussion. In a situation, the evaluator gives two or three topics to the group and gives some time normally five minutes to select one from given topic for discussion. This time is outside the discussion frame. If the group is unable to choose a topic, the evaluator may choose a topic for them and go back to the background noting the start time.

Q. How to address the group and other group members?

Ans. If you are initiating the discussion, it is better to address the group as "Friends". Subsequently, if the group has had a round of self-introduction before starting the discussion and you remember the names, you could use names or simply use pronouns like "he" or "she".

Q. A lot to say on the topic?

Ans. GD is limited by time. It calls for your best delivery in a short time. The group would not look upon you favourably if you kept speaking all the time and did not allow others to speak or listen to others. It is a misconception, that the person who talks the most is the one who is judged the best. The quality and not the volume of your contribution is the success factor.

Q. Should I encourage others to speak up?

Ans. Give space for others to speak. If someone has been trying to speak and has a good point but is cut off constantly, you may encourage him/her to continue with it. However; do not point out or directly put someone who is consistently silent on the spot by asking him/her to speak up.

Q. Are the group members supposed to keep track of the time or will the panel keep track of it?

Ans. It would be good if you are conscious of the time, but not to the point of getting so distracted looking at your watch that you do not contribute to the discussion.

Q. Are we allowed to carry a piece of paper during the GD to note down important points?

Ans. Normally; you are, but there may be instances when it is specifically forbidden to carry paper.

Q. Should we begin the GD by appointing a leader amongst ourselves?

Ans. No, you should not. Leadership in a GD is established implicitly through one's performance in a GD.

Q. Should we distribute the total time available to all the participants to ensure that everybody gets a chance to speak?

Ans. Since a GD is not a debate or elocution, the participants should not resort to the strategy of distributing time amongst them.

Q. Can we take a definite stand in the GD and then later on during the GD, switch over to another stand?

Ans. Yes, provided you do it the right way. In a GD it is quite likely that some other participant's counter-argument convinces you to your point. If this happens, then it is best if you accept his argument and explain to the group how your previous argument was true within a narrow range, and how the new argument applies to a broader range. Naturally, it is safer not to make any rash statements for or against a topic before you learn the facts of the argument. Blindly taking a stand will lead you to trouble. This does not mean you should sit on the fence.

You may participate actively by pointing out both sides of the issue reasonably and logically.

Q. If we do not understand the meaning of the topic, should we ask the moderator to explain it to us?

Ans. No. You cannot. Instead of displaying your ignorance in this manner, it is better to wait for some other participant to explain the meaning of the topic. So, listen to the discussion carefully for the first few minutes and when you have figured out what the topic is about, start participating in the discussion.

Q. Are we expected to stick to the normally accepted line of thought or can we come up with something radical?

Ans. By all means you can. It would demonstrate your creativity and originality. Just make sure it is relevant to the topic.

Q. If I feel strongly about an issue, should I voice my feelings?

Ans. It is important to be cool and emotionally objective in a GD. If you react emotionally, you are likely to lose control over yourself during the group discussion. You have to be calm and logical, not emotional in a GD.

Q. Can I use technical terms or jargon, which is clear to me, but not to the group?

Ans. If you have to use technical terms, please do not use abbreviations. After mentioning the term in full take time out to explain to the group what it means. It is quite likely that other participants of the group have a different academic background from you.

Q. Do I begin my participation by requesting the group's permission to do so?

Ans. It is not likely that you will get a chance to ask for such permission. It may also go against you (as appearing weak on your part).

Q. What is the right time to enter a GD to ensure that I am heard properly?

Ans. In any GD, there are crests and troughs during the discussion. The crest is when the noise level is at its peak. The trough is when there is almost total silence. Ideally, you should enter the GD during the trough period. But in competitive GDs, the crests occur more often and troughs may not occur at all. In such cases, you could identify the stages in the GD, where ideas dear to you are being discussed and enter the GD irrespective of the noise level.

Q. How do I participate when the noise level is too high?

Ans. You could try the following strategy - Identify the most powerful speaker in the group, and note down the points that he/she is making. The moment the noise level reduces a little, enter supporting the powerful speaker. You will have made a strong ally who will carry you through the noise.

Q. Do I have to be cautious about other participants' feelings (on sensitive issues like religion, caste etc.)?

Ans. You certainly do. Insensitivity to others displays a lack of maturity and viciousness. It will act in your favor.

Q. Is it beneficial to be the first speaker in a group discussion?

Ans. Being the first speaker is a high-risk, high-return strategy. If you can make a good opening statement, which is relevant and sets the tone for the GD, it will go in your favor. If you do this well, you may automatically become the group leader. However, if you bungle it up (by speaking for the sake of speaking, not having anything pertinent to say), it will be remembered and will go against your favour.

Q. How critical is my fluency in English to my performance?

Ans. Command over English is certainly advantageous but will not compensate for a lack of good content. If your content is good, then even if your English might not be great, you must speak it out, rather than be inhibited by lack of good English. You will get credit for the soundness of ideas.

Q. How necessary is it to use examples for illustrating an idea?

Ans. Use of examples is helpful in elaborating your point, and helping others understand your idea better. But please remember to keep it short and simple, because in a competitive GD nobody has the patience to listen to long drawn-out examples.

Q. How much or for how long should I participate?

In a 20-minute GD with 10-12 participants, you should try and participate at least 4 times with each entry lasting not less than 25-30 seconds. You could participate more depending on your comfort level and the need for participation.

Q. Is it good to be humorous in a GD?

Ans. This depends on the situation. In a GD that is fairly relaxed, it may be acceptable. But in a competitive situation, where the participants are tensed up, your attempts at humor may fall flat.

Q. Should we make an interim summary?

Ans. An interim summary is a way of directing the group mid-way through the GD. It helps the group to pick out and focus on the most important points and thus use the remaining time more effectively. However, it is not necessary to make an interim summary, if the discussion is already well focused.

Q. What do I do if someone else has already said what I wanted to say?

Ans. You have two choices:

Firstly, agree with the point made by that person and add to it by displaying the applicability of the argument to different situations. By doing this you will have broadened the scope of the argument.

Secondly, drop the point and think of fresh points. To avoid getting into a situation where someone else has already spoken your points, do speak up in the first 4-5 minutes of the GD. If you wait longer, it is almost inevitable that someone would have spoken your points.

Q. Is the use of slang/colloquialism permitted?

Ans. It is best to avoid using slang.

Q. How is aggression taken and measured in a GD?

Ans. The moment you notice people reacting to you negatively or strongly, you may take it that you are being too aggressive. The degree of the reaction is the measure of your aggression.

Q. What level of aggression is seen as acceptable?

Ans. There is a very thin line between aggression and assertiveness. You should always aim to sound assertive and not stubborn.

Q. Is it true that the person who speaks the most in a GD is the most successful one?

Ans. This is a myth. Generally, the person who has a sound knowledge of the topic and is a clear thinker speaks more. This leads the students to believe that whoever speaks most is successful. But just speaking for the sake of speaking will not take you far.

Q. Will I be quizzed about my (or others') participation in the GD?

Ans. You may be. Therefore, it helps to be alert all through the GD.

Q. What is the level of accuracy desired in the facts and figures you quote during the GD?

Ans. An error margin of 5% is acceptable.

Q. Is motivating other people in the group to speak looked upon favourably?

Ans. Depends on how it is done. If you openly request someone to speak, you may be putting the other person in a difficult spot, and the evaluators will not look that upon favorably. It is therefore better to use other means of motivation, such as agreeing with a halting speaker, adding on to their points, implicitly supporting and giving them direction.

Q. Does the moderator have any biases or preconceived notions about the topic?

Ans. Ideally; the moderator is supposed to be unbiased and neutral. But being a human being, the moderator cannot be free from bias.

Since this is not a factor within your control, there isn't much point losing sleep over it.

Q. Can we expect the moderator to stop or cut short the GD much before the stipulated time is over?

Ans. This may happen if the GD becomes too noisy and if the level of discussion deteriorates abysmally.

Q. Can I be aggressive with a lady participant?

Ans. A GD is not the place to demonstrate chivalry. Being rude to any participant (male or female) is downright unacceptable. You need not extend any special privileges to a lady.

Q. Is it all right to ask pointed questions to other participants during a GD?

Ans. It is alright to ask questions for clarification but not to play the devil's advocate and prove them wrong. By playing the devil's advocate you hamper the flow of the GD. The pointed questions unsettle the other participant and the quality of the GD deteriorates. This would reflect badly on you and will go against your favour.

Q. Is it necessary that a group should conclude in the stipulated time?

Ans. Ideally; a group is supposed to conclude. Normally the time constraints do not allow the group to do so.

Q. Is an end-summary essential?

Ans. No. If the group has not concluded, then it would be good if someone puts the whole discussion into perspective by summarizing. But if there isn't sufficient time, a summary may be avoided.

Q. Do we have to write a synopsis of the GD once it is over?

Ans. Some institutes insist on this, but it is not universal.

Q. Is voting an acceptable method of reaching a consensus?

Ans. Not certainly. A GD is not a debate.

Q. How should a group select a topic if asked to?

Ans. The group should brainstorm for about two minutes and narrow down the list of topics to 3-4. After this the group should prioritize them based on the comfort level and ease of discussion of the topics. This could be done by asking each participant to rank the 4 topics and the most popular choice should be taken.

Q. Are the topics decided on the basis of the academic background of the participant?

Ans. No. Topics are usually general in nature to give a level playing field to everyone.

Q. What do I do if one member is very stubborn and aggressive?

Ans. Ignore him and address the other members of the group. Be assertive and tell him that his argument is faulty. Point out to him that his point is well taken and that the group must progress further by discussing the ideas presented by others.

Q. What are the acceptable ways of interrupting somebody else, so that I may make my point?

Ans. You can interrupt in any of the following ways:

"Excuse me, but I feel that what you are saying isn't universally true ..."

"Yes, I agree with your idea, and I would like to add on to it ..."

"Yes, I think you are right when you say that, but could you clarify what if ....?"

Chapter 4

How to Prepare for Group Discussion?

To excel in Group Discussion, it needs preparation. Group Discussion gives an insight into a person performing in real real-life situation along with team members. To make sure you are prepared for group discussion, there are several guidelines one must follow. In the foregoing paragraphs, strategies for preparation are indicated.

1. Increase your knowledge Quotient (KQ):

Knowledge gives the 'content' in a discussion – without good content, you cannot score well. You are required to talk in GD, but a talk that doesn't contain substantial value doesn't hold any meaning. Prepare for as many GD topics as you can. There are some GD topics of perennial interest. You shall not miss the basic economy-related topics, stock markets, inflation, export-import, inflation, globalization, employment scenario etc.

Read Widely. Reading is the first and the most crucial step in preparation. Being an avid reader will help you in group discussions. The more you read, the better you are in your thoughts, remotely it reflects in your personality. While you may read anything to everything, you must ensure that you are in good touch with current affairs, debates and hot topics of discussion and also with the latest in the IT, business and industry. Read both for the thoughts as well as for data. Read multiple viewpoints on the same topic and then create your point of view with rationale. Also, create answers for counter-arguments for your point of view.

Reading is a never-ending process. The more you read, the clearer you are in your thoughts. Many times, it has been seen that candidates either keep mum or repeat a point again and again during a GD. This happens due to a lack of assimilation of knowledge. It is very essential to prepare notes about various topics or information and gather facts as well as data/statistics. Also, read multiple viewpoints on the same topic and then try to create your point of view using your analytical skills. Watching TV channels and the internet (mostly news-related websites) are useful for this. Assimilation of knowledge in the form of notes or points will help you many times before actually appearing for GD.

Adequate knowledge of subject matters is essential. At the same time, have to be well aware of the latest happenings around you, not just in the country but around the world as well. If you can memorize some relevant data, it will be an added advantage. With these steer the conversation to whichever direction you want to.

Be Aware of Topics that are repeated. Often, there are topics which re-appear with minute changes and minor variations. Be aware of such topics well in advance so that you have ample time to prepare for the same. For example, the issues of terrorism, gender inequality, poverty, social conflicts, liberalization and privatization, etc. often appear as GD topics. Make sure you know these topics well and can come up with some unique, insightful points along with dates, stating facts.

Update your current affairs. A candidate should have adequate knowledge about current affairs socio-economic issues and their status, political issues and overall general knowledge. Reading newspapers, magazines and books will certainly help in keeping your general knowledge updated.

One must also look for opportunities to discuss these with other similar candidates to prepare well for group discussion. A group discussion requires an in-depth understanding of the various issues related to a topic, as well as the ability to analyse the topic and build arguments.

Make a habit of reading newspapers and magazines. Read newspapers and magazines on current issues, especially the year-end issues that capture the highlights of the year gone by. Also, watch and listen to news and current affairs on news channels. Watch interesting documentaries and profiles on television to get a wider perspective on issues. Opt for magazines that are content-rich and not just full of advertisements.

2. Stock yourself with information:

No one knows what the topic of GD is going to be. Current Affairs is something that you have to be thorough with. Understand the recent crises that the world is reeling under and the latest developmental initiatives.

Historical topics specifically may not be in GD, however; having historical information will help you cite examples and make reference wherever needed.

Sports, Arts & Literature, in these topics, try to have a decent idea about what is popular, who are the leaders in each area, and the latest that has happened in these areas. If the topic for GD is from these areas, then you will be in control of the situation, or else you can use the information to draw references. Data crunching! Do familiarize yourself with important data. Throwing in some data if required in your GD will create an impression among the assessors.

3. Be Natural & Express Yourself:

The best tip is 'to be what you are'. Sailing through GDs successfully is an art too. Don't try to be artificial. Express your views. Knowledge itself is not enough. The next step is to improve your ability to express yourself. One should be well-versed in expressing his/her feelings, emotions and views in front of a group of strangers. Practice ease of expression since clarity, brevity and choice of words are keenly observed by evaluators. This can be easily done by regular GD preparation among groups of friends classmates or even family members. You can practice speaking in a GD scenario by forming a discussion group which meets every day and takes up a topic for discussion.

4. Mock GD Practice:

Practice brings perfection. Let's start from ground zero. GD preparation can be started among your friends. One should take GD as a meaningful discussion among friends. Each friend has his own opinion on a particular topic. You just need to listen to everyone's point of view and also properly express yours to enhance your GD preparation.

Take every opportunity to take part in mock GDs with full preparations. Join a group of 8 to 10 people and select the topic for group discussion. Try to initiate the GD yourself and start making small contributions to GD. Prepare questions to ask or agree with another speaker's remarks. Try to create a harmonious environment during the practice of mock GD, this will help you in building leadership traits in you.

Form a Discussion Group of friends or colleagues. If you have a group of like-minded friends, you can have a mock group discussion where you can learn from each other through giving and receiving feedback. Create an informal GD group and meet regularly to discuss and exchange feedback. This is the best way to prepare. This would give you a good idea about your thoughts and how well can you convince. Remember, you must be able to express your thoughts well. The better you perform in these mocks the better would be your chances to perform on the final day. Also, try to interact and participate in other GD groups. This will develop in you a skill to discuss with unknown people as well.

The group shall select topics for discussion. It will help you and everyone, to express their respective views on subjects in formal situations. It will help in improving your thinking, listening and speaking skills. It would also enhance your confidence level to present you in a structured set-up. The core mantra for the Group Discussion preparation strategy is to participate in as many practice GDs as possible before you attend the actual GD round.

5. Start Self Practising

After observing what others are practising, a candidate must practise the same to improve discussion skills. One can start with a group of friends and practise on a given topic. Accumulation of knowledge and observation can give you an edge over others only when you practise it in advance before finally appearing for a group discussion. You may also consult an experienced person, ask him if he can guide you or ask your friend to point out your shortcomings. Practise will certainly enhance your knowledge and the ways to conduct yourself in group discussions.

6. Work on your Communication Skills:

You should be well-versed in your communication skills. Inculcate the good habit of structuring your thoughts and presenting them logically. Writing essays on a variety of topics is good practice in developing thought structure. You should have a good vocabulary and a decent command over English. Much before your actual group discussion, rehearse well. You can sit with a group of friends and choose a topic and indulge in a friendly banter. Not only will this increase your knowledge, you will be a better speaker by the time it is time for your GD.

7. Develop Listening Skills:

For making effective Communication, good Listening Skill is a must. Do you listen to others? How do you handle points of view different from yours? Are you able to get across your point of view without appearing to be trying too hard? Communication is perhaps the most critical attribute of the modern officer and executive. These include listening and articulation skills. Moderators look for the candidate's keenness and ability to listen to others – mature managers are very good listeners because every time you listen, you learn. Train you to be a good listener – develop the patience to listen attentively. Acknowledge that everyone has something valuable to say. When speaking in a GD, your job is to articulate your point of view in a way that is easy for others to comprehend.

8. Tutorials & Seminars:

Don't miss any chance to be a part of a GD round at any Institute. Try to learn from each experience during your GD preparation Attend as many seminars and tutorials as possible and notice what other students do. Observe and ask yourself: How do other students make critical comments? How do they ask questions? How do they disagree with or support arguments? What special phrases do they use to show politeness even when they are voicing disagreement? How do they signal to interrupt, ask a question or make a point?

Chapter 5
Do's & Don's in GD

DO'S IN GD

1. Remain as natural as possible. Do not try and be someone you are not. Be yourself.

2. The evaluator wants to hear you speak. You must speak. Speak clearly. Speak politely and clearly. Use simple and understandable words while speaking. Remember that a discussion is not an argument. Learn to disagree politely.

3. Take time to organize your thoughts. Think of what you are going to say.

4. Work out strategies to help you make an entry. Initiate the discussion or agree with someone else's point and then move on to express your views.

5. If you do not give valuable insights during the discussion, all your efforts to initiate the discussion will be in vain.

6. Your body language says a lot about you – your gestures and mannerisms are more likely to reflect your attitude than what you say. Be aware of your body language when you are speaking.

7. Language skills are important only to the effect of how you get your points across clearly and fluently. Keep eye contact while speaking:

8. Be assertive not dominating; try to maintain a balanced tone in your discussion and analysis.

9. Always be polite: Try to avoid using extreme phrases like: `I strongly object' or `I disagree'. Instead try phrases like: `I would like to share my views on...' or `One difference between your point and mine...' or "I beg to differ with you".

10. Allow others to speak. Be receptive to others' opinions and do not be abrasive or aggressive.

11. Initiate the GD. Initiating the GD is a big plus. But keep in mind – Initiate the group discussion only when you understand the GD topic clearly and have some topic knowledge. Speaking without proper subject knowledge is a bad impression.

12. Make sure to keep the discussion on track. If by any means the group is distracting from the topic or goal then simply take initiative to bring the discussion on the track. Make all group members aware that you all need to come to some conclusion at the end of the discussion. So, stick to the topic.

13. Positive attitude. Be confident. Keep positive body language. Show interest in the discussion.

14. Speak sensibly. Don't worry even if you speak less. Your thoughts should be sensible and relevant instead of irrelevant speech. Speak pleasantly and politely to the group.

15. Listen carefully to others: Speak less and listen more! Pay attention while others are speaking. This will make coherent discussion and you will get involved in the group positively. You will surely make people agree with you.

16. No need to go into many details. Some basic subject analysis is sufficient. No need to mention exact figures while giving any reference. You have limited time so be precise and convey your thoughts in short and simple language. Interact with every team member while speaking.

17. Formal dressing. Do not take it casually. No fancy and funny dressing. You should be comfortable while speaking in a group. Positive gestures and body language will make your work easy.

18. Respect the contribution of every speaker. Think about your contribution before you speak. How best can you answer the question/ contribute to the topic? Try to stick to the discussion topic. Don't introduce irrelevant information. Agree with and acknowledge what you find interesting.

19. Progress by own merit. Do not try to make participants small to make yourself large.

20. Not to bother of evaluator. If you impress the group, the evaluator will automatically be impressed.

21. Share your courage. Keep your fear to yourself, but; share your courage with others.

22. Body language. Smiling and nodding are positive body language. Nonverbal communication is adding to one's presentation.

23. Look interested by eye Contact. Try to look interested in GD, by frequent eye contact to persons to whom you are speaking who are speaking to. This will reflect that you are actively listening and acknowledging.

24. Handle by poise. How a person handles a situation is more important than the situation itself. The poise is important. When a man is wrong but does not want to admit it, he is always angry.

26. Clarity. True conversation is saying all that should be said, and that only.

27. Comrades. Do not walk in front of anyone. He may not follow you. Do not walk behind anyone. He may not be willing to lead you. Just walk beside him and be his friend.

DON'TS DURING GD

Many candidates, despite speaking assertively and clearly, are not able to secure expected good marks in group discussions. As a result, they are not selected. Some minor mistakes, which are not kept in mind, perhaps cost the candidate then ouster from the competition.

Here some don'ts are given which every candidate must keep in mind during group discussion.

1. Don't speak just to increase speaking time. Don't worry even if you speak less. Your thoughts should be sensible and relevant instead of irrelevant speech.

2. Don't be too aggressive during group discussions even if you disagree with someone. Express your feelings calmly and politely.

3. Be confident, don't try to dominate anyone. In GD, the candidate is judged by his verbal and non-verbal gestures. Thus, one must speak confidently.

4. Don't indulge in any argument during group discussions, or shout at anyone. This will just earn you negative points.

5. Some people do not want to listen to what others have to say. This attitude may hurt your communication skills. So, listen to the thoughts of every candidate very carefully.

6. Don't interrupt anyone while he/she is speaking. Every candidate may have different thoughts or opinions and may try to present a solution from their perspective.

Don't start speaking until you have clearly understood and analyzed the subject.

Don't lose your temper.

Don't Shout. Use a moderate tone and medium pitch.

Don't use too many gestures when you speak. Gestures like finger-pointing and table thumping can appear aggressive.

Don't dominate the discussion. Confident speakers should allow quieter students a chance to contribute.

Don't draw too much on personal experience or anecdotes. Although some tutors encourage students to reflect on their own experiences, remember not to generalize too much.

Don't interrupt. Wait for a speaker to finish what they are saying before you speak.

Don't lose your cool if anyone says anything you object to. The key is to stay objective.

Don't take the discussion personally.

Don't try to dominate anyone.

DON'T interrupt anyone in between while speaking. Even if you don't agree with his/her thoughts do not snatch their chance to speak. Instead, make some notes and clear the points when it's your turn.

Don't be too aggressive if you are disagreeing with someone. Express your feelings calmly and politely.

Don't speak just to increase your speaking time.

DON'T criticize on religion. Do not get personal with anyone. Never try to bluff.

Chapter 6
What GD Panel Looks For?

You should be seen and heard while making a presentation. The evaluator will notice you if you display making a positive contribution. The panel will observe the ideas put forward by you. Your deliberation should be effective and meaningful and not sidelining the main issue. It has to be sensible and relate to the topic. You shall present your knowledge of the topic logically. You should have an effective combination of knowledge and skills. Knowledge comprises understanding of the topic assigned and also a good level of awareness of the world around us.

Panel looks if you are interested in listening to others viewpoints about the same subject and whether you are able to conduct yourself with grace in a group situation. In case of discussion on a case study, your approach to the case study will be observed keenly by the evaluators. You shall make an attempt to achieve a consensus, if you do not succeed in it or not. Your attempt for consensus matters.

The panel will judge team members for their alertness and presence of mind, problem-solving abilities, ability to work as a team without alienating certain members, and creativity. The selection panel expects teamwork. Today team players are considered more important than individual contributors. Hence the potential to be a leader is evaluated and also ability to work in a team is tested. The evaluators generally assess the oral competence of a candidate in terms of team listening, appropriate language, clarity of expression, positive speech attitudes and adjustments, clear articulation, and effective non-verbal communication.

The selection panel notes the differences in the amount of participation of the members. They observe the silent spectators, the ever-dominating but not contributing much, members who participate actively exhibiting their knowledge and the moderate ones. Your ability lies in analyzing the problem well and making others endorse your view. Finally, while appreciating others' points of view, you should effectively present yours without contradicting other's opinions. Your ability to convince the team is your success.

You shall display some managerial leadership qualities. This is most important. You should be seen to possess leadership qualities which you have to display, if you have to sell your ware.

In the GD, the aim is to judge the participants based on personality, knowledge content, communicative ability to present the knowledge and leadership skills. Let us discuss the salient aspects of these.

Personality:

Even before one starts communicating, the impression is created by the appearance, body language, eye contact, mannerisms used etc. The attire of a participant creates an impression; hence it is essential to be dressed appropriately. The hairstyle also needs to suit the occasion. Other accessories also have to be suitable for the occasion.

In the entire participation in the GD, body language has an important role in the impact created. Body language, a non-verbal communication skill gives important clues to personality assessment. It includes the posture of a person, the eye contact and the overall manner in which one moves and acts.

The facial expression helps to convey attitudes like optimism, self-confidence and friendliness. As non-verbal cues such as eye contact, body movements, gestures, facial expressions, and so on can speak louder than words, examiners closely watch the non-verbal behaviour of candidates.

The panel generally evaluates the body language cues of candidates to determine personality factors such as nervousness, cooperation, frustration, weakness, insecurity, self-confidence, defensiveness, and so forth. So, it is important to be careful while using non-verbal messages.

Knowledge Content:

Content is a combination of knowledge and ability to create coherent, logical arguments on the basis of that knowledge. Also, a balanced response is what is expected and not an emotional response. In a group discussion, greater the knowledge of the subject more confident and enthusiastic would be the participation. Participants need to have a fair amount of knowledge on a wide range of subjects. The discussion of the subject must be relevant, rational, convincing and appealing to the listeners.

People with depth and range of knowledge are always preferred by dynamic companies and organizations. The topics for GD tests may include interesting and relevant ideas about social, economic, political or environmental problems; controversial issues, innovations or case studies. One needs to keep abreast with national and international news, political, scientific, economic, and cultural events, key newsmakers etc. This has to be supplemented by one's own personal reasoning and analysis. Subject knowledge also includes the ability to analyze facts or information systematically and to place them in the context of the framework of one's personal experiences.

Communication Skills:

First and foremost, feature of communication skills is that it is a two-way process. Hence the communicator has to keep in mind the listeners and their expectations. The participants need to observe the group dynamics. Since GD tests one's behavior as well as one's influence on the group, formal language and mutual respect are obvious requirements.

One may not take strong views in the beginning itself but wait and analyze the pros and cons of any situation. If one needs to disagree, learn to do so politely. One can directly put forward the personal viewpoint also. One may appreciate the good points made by others; can make a positive contribution by agreeing to and expanding an argument made by another participant. An idea can be appreciated only when expressed effectively. A leader or an administrator has the ability to put across the idea in an influential manner.

Since oral skills are used to put across ideas, the ability to speak confidently and convincingly makes a participant an impressive speaker. The members of the selection committee closely evaluate the oral communication skills of the candidates.

Effective communication would imply the use of correct grammar and vocabulary, the right pitch, good voice quality, clear articulation, logical presentation of the ideas and above all, a positive attitude. It is expected that there are no errors of grammar or usage and that appropriate words, phrases etc. are used. One should try to use simple and specific language. One should avoid ornamental language. Clarity of expression is one of the important criteria of communication. When there is clarity of thinking, there is clarity in the usage of language. Positive Speech Attitudes is another criterion of evaluation in the GD whereby the participant's attitude towards listeners including other group members is judged. The temperament of the participant is also evaluated through the speech pattern.

Lack of active listening is often a reason for failure of communication. In the GD, participants often forget that it is a group activity and not a solo performance as in elocution. By participating as an active listener, he or she may be able to contribute significantly to the group deliberations. The listening skills are closely linked to the leadership skills as well.

Leadership Skills:

Employers today look for candidates who can work in a team-oriented environment. The success of any group depends to a large extent upon the leader. One of the common misconceptions about leadership is that the leader is the one who controls the group. There are different approaches to the concept of leadership. By studying the personality traits of great leaders or actual dimensions of behavior to identify leadership one can learn to cultivate essential traits of leaders. In a GD, a participant with more knowledge, one who is confident, and one who can find some solution to the problem and display initiative and responsibility will be identified as the leader.

A candidate's success in a GD test will depend not only on his or her subject knowledge and oral skills but also on his/her ability to provide leadership to the group. Adaptability, analysis, assertiveness, composure, self-confidence, decision-making, discretion, initiative, objectivity, patience, and persuasiveness are some of the leadership skills that are useful in proving oneself as a natural leader in a GD.

The leader in a group discussion should be able to manage the group despite differences of opinion and steer the discussion to a logical conclusion within the fixed time limit. The panel will assess whether each participant is a team player who can get along with people or an individualist who is always fighting to save his/her ego. GD participants need several team management skills to function effectively in a team. Some of the skills needed to manage a group effectively include adaptability, positive attitude, cooperation, and coordination.

The candidate who scores higher in displaying abilities: Ability to work in a team, Communication skills, Reasoning ability, Leadership Skills, Initiative Assertiveness, Flexibility Creativity, Ability to think on one's feet has a has a higher chance of being selected.

Chapter 7
Which Role to Display in GD?

The roles displayed by candidates in GD can be either Negative Roles or Positive roles. A candidate may play more than one role in the same GD. The negative roles should be avoided and as soon as you realize that you are being seen as a negative role player you should try to mend your ways and switch over to a positive role at the earliest. The more a candidate sticks to the positive roles the better the chances of his or her selection. The highly recommended role is that of Natural Leader.

NEGATIVE ROLES: ANTAGONISER:

This person assigns himself or someone else as the chairman of the group at the start of the discussion, starts giving orders to others, is a poor listener, tries to control the time duration each candidate speaks, shouts at others when they don't listen to him/her, flaunts his past experience or education qualification, is dogmatic in expressing his views, uses intimidating gestures while talking and so on. If you play this role, you are sure to be out of the game.

NEGETIVE ROLES: FICKLER:

He or she speaks for the sake of speaking, agrees with anyone and everyone, contradicts his statements, fails to present his ideas cohesively, lacks rhythm in his speech, gets too emotional during the speech, abruptly starts talking when others are presenting their views or abruptly stops halfway while talking.

NEGATIVE ROLES: STUPID:

Takes no initiative to present his/her views, is nervous, does not take any responsibility, is devoid of ideas, tries to find excuses for not contributing, pretends to be a good listener and just repeats what other members said thus not contributing anything positive to the group.

POSITIVE ROLES: INITIATOR:

The initiator as the name suggests is the person who sets the ball rolling. One must start the discussion if he/she has mastery over the subject being discussed or if he/she believes that she can do justice to the subject topic. Starting the discussion just for the sake of it may put you in soup. When you start the discussion there are very high chances that you get enough time to speak before you are interrupted by others. During this period chances of chaos are very low and the evaluator has his full focus on you. You if you speak well, you score some brownie points there, but if you don't meet the evaluator's expectation you are likely to give a bad impression and remember the evaluator has his undivided attention to what you are saying.

POSITIVE ROLES: CO-ORDINATOR:

The co-coordinator usually makes sure that every who is willing to speak gets a chance to speak. He is the one who takes the group out of chaos in case of a heated argument between two group members. He is usually the one who summarizes the discussion at the end and in between helps others in putting the thought across. This is a very risky role to play as other candidates may not be happy as you trying to co-ordinate the whole event and present yourself as the leader of the group. If you have the human tacking skills and knowledge on the subject being discussed you are sure shot winners if you play this role.

HIGHLY RECOMMENDED ROLE: NATURAL LEADERS

Speaks elegantly on the subject, does not argue with others just for the sake of it, and influences others with his mannerisms and speech. Listens to what others are saying, accepts and encourages others to come out with different viewpoints, and provides relevant data and information to help others convey their points. Others are comfortable to follow the guidelines laid by him. The co-coordinator usually looks to him at time of need and when the situation gets out of control. This role can be adopted by a person who has in-depth knowledge, a balanced personality, clear thoughts and the ability to convey his thoughts in words.

Chapter 8
Common Mistakes of Participants

1. Emotional outburst: Ms Susan was offended when one of the male participants made a general statement about women while explaining his point of view. When Susan got an opportunity to speak, instead of focusing on the topic, she vented her anger by accusing the other candidate of being a male chauvinist and went on to defend women in general.

Susan made the following mistakes:

Her behaviour was perceived as immature and de-motivating to the rest of the team. By her emotional outburst what Susan did do in GD? It led her to deviate from the subject, treat the discussion as a forum to air her views, lose objectivity and make personal attacks.

2. Quality Vs Quantity: Mr. Michael believed that the more he would speak, the more likely he would get through the GD. He deliberately interrupted other members at every opportunity and sometimes without opportunity. He annoyed and angered others including the evaluator. He did this, so often; that the other candidates got together to prevent him from participating in the rest of the discussion.

Michael made the following mistakes:

He knew when to mistake but he did not know when not to speak. He did not realize that success depends on quality, not quantity. He attempted to dominate the group. Domination is frowned upon. Assessment is not on your too much speaking but on your communication, cooperation, listening, teamwork and leadership skills. Evaluation is based on quality, and not on quantity. Your contribution must be relevant. The mantra is "Contributing meaningfully to the team's success."

3. Showing of excessive knowledge: The topic was "Is reservation in parliament seats against democracy and secularism". David became over jubilant no sooner the topic was announced. He started projecting his vast knowledge of the topic. Whatsoever he said had some statics data. He even interrupted, corrected and supplemented other speakers by citing data like so many per cent of parliament seats, so many members of parliament, and so many constituencies, so many seats etc. The other candidates took that he was bluffing and giving false data. They even laughed at him. After some time, they completely ignored him.

David made the following mistakes:

He too much attempted to show off his knowledge. Even if, he had enough knowledge, he should have exercised restraint and spoken for a reasonable length of time instead of long deliberation. He should have expressed his willingness to listen to others.

4. Hurry to get noticed: James knew that no sooner, the topic was announced, everyone would rush to start. He too wanted to be the first one to start. The topic was "Is a scheme of subsidy on housing is for below LIP? Low-Income Group"" James did not listen to LPL (meaning Low Income Group) and started speaking that it would benefit the entire citizen equally. However, he was interrupted and corrected by fellow participants and scored all the points.

James made the following mistakes:

He forgot that to start first, though rewarding is costly, high- risk high-gain exercise. He initiated without listening and understanding the topic. Had he done so, he would have presented his views differently. In case he failed to listen or was not very clear about the topic, he should have waited for someone to start first. On listening to that speaker, he would realize his misunderstanding and deliberated meaningfully.

5. Fear and nervousness: John was nervous at the outset that participants might laugh at him if he made a wrong point or his sentences had grammatical errors. After listening to other people, he

thought all others were better than him. He withdrew himself to silence and did not speak even one participant invited him to speak.

John made the following mistakes:

He did not realize that unless he speaks, he cannot be evaluated. Evaluation is the job of the evaluator. He evaluated himself as the most inferior than others. He focused on his weakness instead of strength. His body language showed "I am over-awed by others".

6. Egotism & Showing off: Rohan was happy to have got a group discussion topic he had prepared for. He started projecting his vast knowledge of the topic as if he was lecturing in class room. Every other sentence of his contained statistical data – " 15% of companies; 28.07% of parliamentarians felt that...; I recently read in a Jupiter Report that..." and so on so forth. Soon, the rest of the team either laughed at him or ignored his attempts to enlighten them as they perceived that he was cooking up the data.

Rohan made the following mistakes:

He did not exercise restraint in putting forward data and points. He ended up being frowned upon if you attempted to show off your knowledge. Data and figures need not validate all your statements. It's your analysis and interpretation that are equally important – not just facts and figures. You might be appreciated for your in-depth knowledge. But you will fail miserably in your people relationship skills. Such behaviour indicates how self-centered you are and highlights your inability to work in an atmosphere where different opinions are expressed.

7. Uncontrolled Emotions: The topic of GD was "Role of women as managers." Mr Robert commented that "women are very often submissive". This offended Miss Patricia She did not react immediately. When she took her chance to speak, she vigorously attacked Mr. Robert by branding him as women chauvinist and spoke in favour of women in general.

The mistakes Miss Patricia committed:

She took the general comment of Robert as personal. She deviated from the topic and could not make any meaningful contribution to GD. In an answer to a relevant statement, she made a direct personal attack, which was irreverent and unwanted. She spoiled the atmosphere of GD and the morale of the team.

8. Get noticed – But for the right reasons: George knew that everyone would compete to initiate the discussion. So as soon as the topic – "Discuss the negative effects of joining the BRICKS" – was read out, he began talking. In his anxiety to be the first to start speaking, he did not hear the word "negative" in the topic. He began discussing how the country had benefited by joining BRICKS, only to be stopped by the evaluator, who then corrected his mistake as the GD would have been misdirected.

George made the following mistakes:

False starts are extremely expensive. They cost you your elimination. It is very important to listen and understand the topic before you air your opinions. Spending a little time analyzing the topic may provide you with insights which others may not have thought about. Use a pen and paper to jot down your ideas. Listen! It gives you the time to conceptualize and present the information in a better manner. Some mistakes are irreparable. Starting the group discussion with a mistake is one such mistake unless you have a great sense of humour.

10. Managing one's insecurities: Ms Barbara was very nervous at the outset. She thought that some of the other candidates were exceptionally good. She contributed little to the discussion. Even when she was asked to comment on a particular point, she preferred to remain silent. The mistakes Miss Barbara committed:In the end, she felt that she had better facts to place in GD, but; her nervousness spoiled her chance. So, one has to manage his or her insecurities in GD.

11. Look at you: Mr William was the last person to come in the room as he was stuck in traffic. Everyone was in their seats when he

entered the room. He was the last person to enter the room. When he entered, everyone stared at him. He felt relieved noticing that the evaluator had not come. William noticed that candidates were giving strange expressions and even smiling. The girl candidates were avoiding to at look at him. It was only when the evaluator called him and asked him to fasten his jig. Then only he realized that why the candidates were smiling. William committed the following mistakes: He did not start early enough to reach on time keeping a note of possible traffic congestion. In a hurry, he failed to check his dress. He failed to handle the situation by saying excuse me. Such carelessness shows that you cannot manage your get up and behaviour on such an important occasion as GD.

Chapter 9

How to lead in GD.?

We are going discuss the following aspects of how to lead in GD.
1. Readiness for GD.
2. Taking the initiative to initiate GD.
3. How to Initiate GD & Lead a Discussion?
4. Don't Miss - Take Your Opportunity to Speak.
5. Communicating your views.
6. Proper Non-Verbal Clues.
7. Display Leadership.
8. Speaking.
9. Avoid Diversion and Distraction.
10. GD Closing: How to summarise the GD?

1. Readiness for GD.

Let us start this chapter with Readiness for GD. You need to look impressive, well-groomed and confident. On the day of GD, dress in comfortable clothes. Dress formally. Always dress in formal. Wearing a good combination of a dark and light outfit is a good idea. Ensure your clothes are well-ironed. Footwear is polished, neat & tidy. For men, if you wear a black belt ensure you are in black footwear. Avoid too much jewellery during interviews or group discussions.

Always carry a pen and piece of paper or notebook along with you whenever you go for GD and use them unless it is not allowed to do so. This allows you to refer to what others have said previously.

Sit comfortably and prepare yourself mentally. Make sure you are comfortable where you're sitting and you're not moving and fidgeting all the time. Sit with a straight and confident posture. Don't play with your hair, or rub your together or any other thing that shows you're nervous.

First of all, you need to realize that a GD is exactly what the term itself says. Prepare yourself mentally to speak in front of everyone. It's just a discussion! Mentally visualize yourself as succeeding and you will succeed. Be confident but avoid being overconfident. Be positive and prepare your thoughts well. Be as natural as possible. Do not try to be someone you are not. Be yourself. In an attempt to be someone else, your opinions will not be portrayed.

1. Taking the initiative to initiate GD:

Initiating a GD is sometimes very profitable, but also involves a high risk. When you initiate a GD, you not only grab the opportunity to speak, but you also grab the attention of the evaluator and that of your fellow participants.

If you can make a favourable first impression with your subject matter and communication skills at this time, it will help you score good marks overall.

When you start a GD, you are responsible for putting it into the right perspective or frame of reference. So initiate a GD only if you have in-depth knowledge about the topic and know exactly what you want to say.

When you start a GD, you are responsible for putting it into the right perspective or frame of reference. So initiate a GD only if you have in-depth knowledge about the topic and know exactly what you want to say.

Different techniques can be used to initiate a GD and make a first good impression on others. These may include the following

1. It is always considered beneficial to start a group discussion with a famous quote for a topic like 'Need for Good Leaders in India', one could start with Napolean Bonaparte's famous saying, 'A leader is a dealer in hope'.

2. If the topic of group discussion is 'Capital Punishment should be Banned', one can initiate the discussion by defining 'Capital Punishment'.

3. Asking a question and replying by the same person is another technique of initiation for example if the topic of discussion is 'Should India have war with Pakistan'? one may start group discussion by asking, "Do we achieve anything by war"?

4. If one makes a shocking statement to start a group discussion, this grabs immediate attention. For instance, for the topic 'Road Accidents on Preventable' a shocking statement for initiation can be "Are you all aware that the number of deaths due to road accidents in India is much higher than the world average"? we need to ask 'why'?

5. If you initiate group discussion with the help of some facts, data or figures, you must make sure that you are correct.

Keep the following points in mind during this stage

(i) If you have not been able to initiate the discussion, do not forget to put forward your views in this part of GD.

(ii) Try to speak to the point and express one's contentions clearly and concisely in an assertive way.

(iii) Do not repeat your arguments.

(iv) Try to present your view along with correct facts data or examples. Do not ever try to give facts which are not correct.

(v) Try to complete your thoughts in the stipulated time.

Try to be the first and the last to speak. Try to initiate the Group Discussion, if possible. By taking the initiative, you will be giving a structure to the discussion and defining how the discussion will progress. This will exhibit your quality as a person who can facilitate actions by breaking the ice. When you initiate a GD, you not only grab the opportunity to speak, but you also grab the attention of the panellist and your fellow candidates.

Many candidates wish to go for the GD opening or being the first speaker because that instantly grabs the attention of the Observers and gives some extra points to the candidate. Initiating a GD is a high profit-high loss strategy. If you can make a favourable first impression with your content and communication skills after you initiate a GD, it will help you sail through the discussion. A little word of caution here, attempt to lead, only if you have a fair amount of knowledge about the topic and you know exactly what you are speaking.

But if you initiate a GD and stammer, stutter, or quote wrong facts and figures, the damage might be irreparable. If you initiate a GD impeccably but don't speak much after that, it gives the impression that you started the GD for the sake of starting it or getting those initial kitty of points earmarked for an initiator! When you start a GD, you are responsible for putting it into the right perspective or framework. So, initiate one only if you have in-depth knowledge about the topic at hand. If you take the initiative of being the lead and somehow you are unable to pull it through, then it will backfire completely. So, act wisely.

GD opening is an art and depends on your confidence and knowledge of the topic. But GD opening can be a two-edged sword, if your content is not up to the mark, then GD opening can become fatal for you and will then have to work extra hard in that GD round to make up for your lost points. Take the move only if you have complete knowledge of the subject. You could grab the opportunity to speak first, don't shy away if you know the topic well. If you are not too familiar with the topic then the wise thing would be to wait and listen attentively to a couple of participants speak and then you could find an opportunity to speak and build on that.

Be confident about yourself and your thought process. You don't have to worry about what anyone thinks of you. Trust your instincts, say what you feel, and say it boldly and clearly. Earn some brownie points by impressing the evaluator.

3. How to Initiate GD & Lead a Discussion?

Listen to the Topic Given During GD Carefully. Once the topic is given the participants are given some time before the discussion is started. Listen to the topic carefully and understand it. Be alert. You should understand what the topic is really about. Sometimes, the topic may be really simple but the manner, in which it is presented to you, can be baffling. When the topic is given, understand the topic carefully. Clarity of the topic is of utmost importance to ensure that you perform well in the GD. Before you start speaking, think through the major issues in the topic in the first two minutes. Start speaking only when you have understood and analyzed the topic.

Opening lines to Initiate Discussion matters a lot. In GD, the group does not have a formal leader; hence one of the participants is expected to take the initiative. Normally, when the panel gives to group a topic and asks to proceed, the discussion takes place. Many times, participants simply keep on sitting. In this, enough time is lost. Here comes the role of a leader, who imitates discussion and deserves credit by panel. To get the GD started, the assertive, natural leader will have to remind the group of its goal and request them to start the discussion without wasting time.

A few examples of the opening lines are given below:

"Well friends, may I request your kind attention? I am sure all of us are keen to begin the GD and complete it within the allotted time. Let me remind you that we have only thirty minutes to complete the task. So, let us get started."

"My dear friends, may I have your attention, please? As you all know, we have to complete the discussion in 30 minutes and we have already used up five minutes. I think we should start the discussion now."

"Hello everybody"! I am sorry to interrupt but I have something very important to say. We are here to discuss the topic — "Human cloning should be banned."—and the time given to us is just 30 minutes. Let us begin, shall we?"

There are different techniques to make a good first impression. One has to choose the one to which he or she is more comfortable. Following are a few such techniques:

Start with quotes: If the topic of a GD is: "Should the Censor Board be abolished?" You could start with a quote like, 'Hidden apples are always sweet'.

For a GD topic like, "Customer is King"; you could quote Sam (Wall-mart) Walton's famous saying, 'There is only one boss: the customer. And he can fire everybody in the company — from the chairman on down, simply by spending his money somewhere else.'

Start a GD by defining *the topic* or an important term in the topic.

For example, if the topic of the GD is "Advertising is a Diplomatic Way of Telling a Lie", why not start the GD by defining advertising as, 'Any paid form of non-personal presentation and promotion of ideas, goods or services through mass media like newspapers, magazines, television or radio by an identified sponsor'?

For a topic like Malthusian Economics, you could start by explaining the definition of the Malthusian Economic Prophecy.

Start by Question: Asking a question is an impact way of starting a GD. It does not signify asking a question to any of the candidates in a GD so as to hamper the flow. It implies asking a question and answering it yourself. Any question that might hamper the flow of a GD or insult a participant or play devil's advocate must be discouraged. Questions that promote a flow of ideas are always appreciated.

For a topic like, "Should Nation go to war", you could start by asking, 'What does war bring to the people of a nation? We have had a few clashes in the past. The pertinent question is: what have we achieved?'

4. Don't Miss - Take Your Opportunity to Speak:

After hearing the topic, try to gather your thoughts on the given topic. Think about the points you're going to say and note them. Make a rough sketch of the points that you would like to speak about. Work out strategies to help you make an entry, initiate the discussion or agree with someone else's point and then move on to express your views. Listen carefully and speak only at the appropriate time. Understand the topic before attempting to contribute. When the matter is quite clear and the GD is in the midst then you should start speaking with new ideas in mind. If you have some confusion then you should wait for some time and let the other speak at first.

Identify the way to enter the Group discussion. In a loud GD where there are three or four aggressive participants, and where a number of people tend to speak at the same time, it becomes difficult for others to get a chance to speak. There is no foolproof solution to this problem. And such a situation is pretty much likely to prevail during the actual GD round that you participate in. However, you must speak. People will ask you to be polite and wait for someone to finish their argument before you start speaking. However, this doesn't work. If you let someone speak, they won't stop until the time for the group discussion is over. So, you need to know how to cheekily take your opportunity to speak. Be polite, but whenever the person speaking pauses somewhere, or has a break in his thought process and takes a second to think, take your chance and put forward your opinion. You don't want to be waiting all the time to just get your turn.

Make the best of this opportunity, the evaluator wants to hear you speak. A GD is a chance to be more vocal. Ensure that you get to speak your point, if the other members hear you, the evaluators will too. Be very sure of what you are speaking. Use easy-to-understand English. Speak loudly and clearly. Talk sense. Avoid superficial talk. Deviating from the main topic or passing strong statements like 'I agree or disagree ...' should be avoided. Your strategy should be to test the waters and make a generic statement relevant to the topic. If you can, back it up with relevant data. You are being heard and judged upon. Use quotes, facts and figures, statements, and everyday life examples to express a clear chain of thoughts. Also, it might leave a good impression on the panel and help you score well.

5. Communicating Your Views:

You may have excellent views on the topic, but are you able to communicate them effectively are the question? When you are talking on the topic, choose your points in a manner that they conveys the depth of knowledge that you possess. Superficial talk is going to be a strict no-no here as the assessors will be easily able to see through.

Understand that the aim is not to speak often or for long periods. The aim is to be precise and clear with your points. Ultimately, the discussion has to conclude and you must strive towards that. As you are gathering thoughts, try to stick to precise and concise thoughts. Remember, when you are communicating, what is more important is what you are communicating rather than how much you are communicating. In a Group Discussion, it is always quality over quantity. Let your views be relevant and to the point. To a great extent, try to do some out-of-the-box thinking so that your view stands out from the rest.

Everybody will state the obvious. So, highlight some points that are not obvious. Don't try to be a part of the crowd. On the contrary, try to be unique, if possible. But that would mean taking a risk. The different perspectives that you bring to the group will be highly appreciated by the panel. Be careful that the "something unique" you say is still relevant to the topic being discussed in the Group Discussion.

You must try to understand the dynamics in the group behavior. Your group behaviour is reflected in your ability to interact with the other members of the group. In a group discussion, try to be in control of the discussion. This is easier said than done, because most of the group members would be trying to do the same. What you can do is follow the discussion keenly and try to pitch in wherever relevant. If you have some good points, try to put them forth and steer the discussion. Do not be aggressive. Do not force your points. If there is a disagreement on the points that you have made, try to counter them with even more valid points. This will not only exhibit your knowledge but also show that you are a good listener. Try to fuel the discussion whenever possible. Give everyone a chance to speak. If someone has not contributed, ask the person to speak up. This will showcase your ability as a team player. You must be mature enough to not lose your temper even if you are proved wrong. You must be patient and balanced.

6. Proper Non-Verbal Clues:

Good Body language and Gestures are very important. Your body language says a lot about you - your gestures and mannerisms are more likely to reflect your attitude than what you say. The panellists observe the way you sit and react in the course of the discussion. Body gestures are very important because your body language says a lot about you. In a GD, sit straight; avoid leaning back onto the chair or knocking the table with a pen or your fingers. Also, do not get distracted easily. For example, if the door in the room you are sitting.

Nonverbal clues include eye contact, body movements, gestures and facial expressions. The panel very keenly watches the nonverbal behaviour of the team. They generally evaluate the body language cues of the team to determine personality factors such as nervousness, cooperation, frustration, weakness, insecurity, self-confidence, defensiveness, etc. A candidate who appears professional is more likely to be noticed by the panel. A confident posture, appropriate facial expressions and meaningful eye contact with the team will create a good expression.

Maintain eye contact with the team, while speaking with the participants. It creates more room for conversation. This helps you to grab the personal attention of every member in the room giving you extra 'brownie points' in the discussion. Also keep nodding, when others speak, it shows receptivity.

7. Display Leadership:

Self-confidence is a quality which helps win the agreement from other participants. In GD, participants can make a favourable and forceful impact on the group by being persuasive and convincing. Do not look back to see who it is, this will show how distracted you are. The leader will promote positive group interactions; point out areas of agreement and disagreement; help keep the discussion on the right track and lead the discussion to a positive and successful conclusion within the stipulated time.

To be persuasive, one has to advance strong, convincing, and logical arguments properly supported by factual data and forceful illustrations. A firm tone and a sober voice would also help in establishing oneself. A leader's ability to convince others and make them accept his/her views and suggestions will establish his/her credentials for leadership. Leaders are characterized by a high level of motivation and can motivate others too. A person with motivation can work hard to do the best job possible and can achieve targets. Team Management skills are important for a leader to manage the members of varied interests. Some of the skills needed to manage a group effectively include adaptability, a positive attitude, cooperation, and coordination.

The ability to analyze a situation is a quality of leadership. Motivate others to speak. It will demonstrate your leadership skills. You may motivate the other team members to speak but you need to identify the right time to do that. Also, don't keep repeating the same thing as you may lose your time to speak and this may show too much of leadership. Be receptive to others' opinions and do not be abrasive or aggressive.

You must be clearly seen to be attempting to build a consensus. Leader contributes meaningfully and helps arrive at a consensus. It is not a platform for you to fight your way through and dominate.

Flexibility and getting with the group are also very important. You can put forward your arguments logically and are a good communicator and also a good listener. The quality of what you said is more valuable than the quantity. There is this myth among many participants that the way to succeed in a group discussion is by speaking loudly and continuously for a long time. One could not be more wrong. You must have meat in your arguments.

Reaching consensus by considering the group opinion will make the GD successful. Assertiveness that is an ability to bring order to the group by handling the conflict is another desirable quality of leadership. Gaining support or influencing colleagues is the two methods to gain consensus. This is widely used by successful corporate leaders. Nobody expects a group of 10 intelligent and assertive people, all with different points of view on a controversial subject, to achieve a consensus. What matters is the fact that whether you can build any kind of consensus or not? Is the whole group going towards a common point or not? Building consensus is given importance in most organizations you will have to work with people in a team, accept joint responsibilities and make decisions as a group. You must demonstrate the fact that you are capable and inclined to work as part of a team.

8. Become an attentive listener:

Be a good listener. Acknowledge that everyone has something valuable to say. Listen carefully and speak only at the appropriate time. In a GD you are required to carefully listen to the other person's thoughts and keep an argument, example or a supportive statement, fact, or example ready to participate in the discussion. This shows how alert you are, and how much importance you give to when someone is putting his or her point forward. This also shows how good a listener you are, at times, things turn up to be a mess when you feel that what is being said is not make sense. Don't get irritated. Remember that you need to be calm and composed. Many times, after a mess happens in a GD, candidates who are calm are selected.

Carefully listen to what others have to say. Just speaking throughout the discussion doesn't make you smart; you should also give others a chance to speak. Try and listen to him/her, and respect their viewpoint too. If the speaker is making contact with you remember to acknowledge him by saying "Yes, you agree" or just by nodding your head, so that the speaker is aware that his listeners are listening to him and paying full attention. This will also show that you are vigilant and are an active participant in the discussion.

9. Speaking:

Adding valuable thoughts pays. Penning the discussion is not the only way of gaining attention and recognition. If you do not give valuable insights during the discussion, all your efforts to initiate the discussion will be in vain. When speaking in a GD, your job is to articulate your point of view in a way that is easy for others to comprehend. Correctly saying what you want to say- speaking effectively and efficiently is very important. Not knowing is not a problem, do not try to bluff. Seek opportunities to discuss these in groups. Talk sense. Avoid superficial talk.

Do not repeat a point, or be lengthy or irrelevant. Also intervene, if someone else is going on an irrelevant track. Put forth your points without being aggressive.

Use effective & apt language. Language skills are important only to the effect of how you get your points across clearly and fluently. The flow of language must be smooth. Use simple language and avoid long winding sentences. Appropriateness of language demands that there should be no errors in grammar. Do not use unfamiliar phrases and flowery language. Be precise. Be polite.

Improve your vocabulary. This does not mean that you use heavy and big words, but it means that you will be able to understand the topic better and contribute effectively. Do not use high vocabulary. Do not use heavy and big words. Use easy-to-understand English. Never use technical language while speaking. Be very sure of what you are speaking. Don't argue, share your views. The argument is an exchange of ignorance. Discussion is an exchange of knowledge.

Try to avoid using extreme phrases like: `I strongly object' or `I disagree'. Instead try phrases like: `I would like to share my views on...' or `One difference between your points and mine...' or "I beg to differ with you".

Speak loudly and clearly. Make sure that you speak loudly and clearly. This is one of the most important things and you could find yourself in difficulty if you do not speak loudly and clearly in a GD.

Maintain a Balance in your Tone. Be assertive not dominating; try to maintain a balanced tone in your discussion and analysis. Besides what you are saying, remember that the panellists are observing your body language as well. If you do not agree with the other student's point of view, do not raise your tone in objection. Listen to his point of view and instead of dismissing it upfront, try and draw a common ground.

Be Patience & Don't shout. Don't lose your cool if anyone says anything you object to. The key is to stay objective. Don't take the discussion personally. Have a solid premise for every argument you make. It is often said – 'Raise the quality of your argument, not your voice." This is what you must follow. Shouting will not get you anything but the frowns of your colleagues and negative marks from the judges. This is not a futile 'Roadies' group discussion you're preparing for! So, just stay a little calm and control your exuberance and excitement. Don't start jumping around like a 5yearold!

Be yourself and do not be arrogant. Body language is important, so be careful while using gestures and do not ever get aggressive. It's a discussion, not a debate. Don't make the group discussion a heated debate. It is supposed to be a calm discussion and that is how it must stay. Don't start cross-questioning every person without putting forward your points on the topic. No matter how you hate a fellow participant's face, don't start fighting with him/her!

Avoid speaking in turn as it leads to an unnatural discussion. Don't speak in a fixed pattern or number. A GD involves a free-flowing exchange of ideas among participants. Even though there will be chaos in most competitive GDs all participants will be keen to be heard. Speak up whenever you get a chance to.

Knowledge about the subject can never be replaced in a GD. No matter how good you might be communicating, if your sentences don't reflect that you are a knowledge bank then it's probably not going to work out. You are required to talk in a GD but inputs that don't contain any substantial value will not help in any way. One has to keep himself updated by knowing what is happening around the globe.

Out of the box thinking, yes! This is something that can help you get further selected because this reflects that you have a different way of looking at things. You need to be creative and have to put points that might amaze the panel. Remember, while working there are times when we need to find solutions to the problem in a better way, thinking out of the box helps you find smart and good solutions at times.

10. Avoid Diversion and Distraction:

Do not allow yourself to be diverted by other people's points. Do not be distracted. Your concentration should be solely on the discussion. Do not be deterred by other member's aggressive or submissive behaviour. Do not be deterred by other member's aggressive or submissive behaviour. Accommodate diverse viewpoints. Do not allow yourself to be diverted by other people's points. Do not be distracted. Your concentration should be solely on the discussion. Do not get excited or aggressive during the discussion. Try to maintain a balanced tone throughout

Do not deliberately try to make eye contact with the evaluator/s. They're not a part of the discussion. Do not try to purposefully look at them to draw their attention. They are smart enough to realize that you are deliberatively attempting to show them your presence instead of actively participating in GD. However, if you happen to have eye contact incidentally with them while speaking gently shift your eyes.

First of all, one should try to make sure that the judges are noticing you. You have to be seen by the evaluating panel to have made a meaningful contribution. You must ensure that everyone in the group listens to you. If the group hears you, so will the evaluator. That does not mean that you shout at the top of your voice and be noticed for the wrong reasons. You have to be assertive. If you are not a very assertive person, you will have to simply learn to be assertive for those 15 minutes. Remember, assertiveness does not mean being arrogant. Arrogant is a different thing.

11. Facilitate others:

Do not just go on and on and on with only your opinionated view. Remember, it is a group discussion. Allow others to speak too. Having said that, ensure that you listen as well and appreciate what others are saying. If you do not agree with someone's point, let them complete it and then raise your objection. Do not interrupt. Accommodate diverse viewpoints. Give due importance to other person views. However, stick to the point you have made. Try to support it with more viewpoints.

Accommodate and appreciate others' views. Respect others for what they are. Learn to be open-minded and recognize the fact that people think differently about issues. Give due importance to other person views. Put forth your points without being aggressive. However, stick to the point you have made. Try to support it with more viewpoints.

Participate and try to contribute throughout the discussion. Do not get excited or aggressive during the discussion. Be an active and dynamic participant. Be assertive yet humble. You need to stick to your values and beliefs but learn to respect the values and opinions of others too. When objecting to a point kept by another speaker, back it up with a solid reason to get the point across. Try and sort out contradictions and arguments. Providing a meaningful direction to the discussion always leaves a good impression on the evaluators.

12. GD Closing: How to summarise the GD?

Summarizing the discussion at the end is called GD closing, which is the most important aspect of GD. When the discussion is about to end or when the topic has been discussed for a reasonable length of time, try to summarise the discussion. If you do this, you will score extra points. This will indicate your analytical skills and also the way you structure your thoughts.

Do not get upset if the group is unable to reach a consensus. In the group, everyone will have somewhat different stands and points on the issue. None expects that a consensus will be arrived at in the light of divergent views in limited-timed discussion. All that is required is an attempt should have been to reach a consensus.

A manager works with a group of people having individual differences in temperament likes and dislikes views etc. Some of them may not agree with a particular point or conclusion. Yet the decision arrived at will be considered as a group decision and the group has to take responsibility for the same despite that one or two members have dissented.

An attempt to reach a consensus is treated as an attempt to work in a team. In summary, cover the following:

1. The issue in brief.
2. The majority point of view.
3. Dissenting viewpoints.
4. Whether the group has been able to reach a consensus or not.

In GD closing, do not merely restate your point of view, also accommodate dissenting viewpoints. If the group did not reach a consensus, say so in your summary or GD closing, but remember, do not force a consensus. Forcing a consensus could end up working against you. All well that ends well, this saying is apt for GD closing. If you have the confidence to summarize the GD i.e., GD closing then

this will result in getting good last minute extra points from the Group
Discussion

Chapter 10

How to Manage Participants Behavior

We are now to discuss the following aspects of how to manage participants' behavior:

1. Types of Participants.
2. Tips to Deal with an Ego Hungry Participants.
3. When & How to Interrupt in GD?
4. Examples of How to Interrupt?
5. Sentences not to be used to interrupt.
6. How to look different?
7. How to Handle Awkward Situation?

1. Types of Participants:

Group Discussion Behavior is peculiar. Members, at sometimes; behave as if they are one person. But; at times, they are emotionally charged and behave violently that they normally would not think of doing individually.

GD participants may consist of three types, which you will come across.

1. Quarrelsome persons: They may shout at, mock or point out on silly matter. Generally; such persons have least knowledge of topic. They will never come to topic of discussion, no matter what you do. Such persons are jealous of you scoring points. They want to disturb discussion, if I can't, let others not.

You can easily spot such person with their mannerism in group. You do not lose any marks for what they say to you. But you lose if you shout back or lose your cool. If you can handle even any of them, you score points. Else, you need not lose your limited time to put your points.

2. Self-centered persons: They believe to score not by their own merit but at the cost of others. They behave as if they are not in group.

They are highly concerned with themselves and self-centered. They try to derail discussion by frequent interruptions, frivolous objections, raising already discussed issue. They display aggressiveness and make unwanted criticism. They boost of themselves to draw attention of others. They crack jokes instead of discussing on topic.

3. Leaders: They have reasonable knowledge of the topic. They support and praise good points rose by others. They avoid confrontation and help in resolving disagreements and conflict between others. They act as tension reliever. They listen to what others have to say. They encourage others who had no opportunity to speak. They initiate group discussion. They encourage others to speak. They are good speakers. They clarify other's point. They lead group discussion in proper direction. Such types of candidates score better marks. Try to have these traits in you and your success is definite.

2. Tips to Deal with an Ego Hungry Participants.

All candidates have a self-interest in GD. Your primary concern is your success not others. So is the case with others. Further every person has an ego. To an ego hungry person, you can satisfy his ego by following steps:

1. Make them feel important. Make him or her feel that you are eager to listen to what they have to say.

2. Always give credit for their suggestions. Make them feel that their suggestions are very useful.

3. Always thank them asking you to explain. This will give you an opportunity to expand your views.

4. Always thank them for giving you an opportunity to speak.

5. Always sincerely defend them when someone tries to ridicule them.

6. Always encourage them to speak by asking for their opinion.

7. Do not stress on winning all the time. Sometimes it is better to move back to go forward.

8. Do not try to correct a person who shows persistent problem behaviour. If you cannot persuade him, isolate him.

3. When & How to Interrupt in GD?

The general rule is that you should not interrupt others while they are speaking. However, if you strictly follow it, you will never get a chance to speak. You have a right to speak for a reasonable length of time. If you are deprived of it, it is better to interrupt. Unskilled interruption will be the irritants, however; if you skillfully, do it, no one will mind it. In fact, no one will notice it.

You can interrupt others by starting with the following words and then immediately thereafter, adding your views:

That's a good idea! However, ...

That's a great idea. But.......

I agree. In addition............

That is, it!

You said it!

Fine!

That is right. But sometimes......

You have a point there. Permit me to elaborate it......

Very correct! But I could add that..........

You are right but you may also like to tell the group that............

Very well said! I would like to supplement it.......

This point needs further elaboration.........

Yes, that is another point.........

You are on the right track. Another important point is that ....

I am glad that you have brought up this point. In fact, ...

4. Examples of How to Interrupt?

Example: 1: In GD, the topic for discussion is "Seniority, not merit, must be a criterion for promotion". Oliver is speaking in favour of seniority for a long.

You need to interrupt him. How to do that? You can say *"Well said. However, there is one other angle to it. Because of computerization, technology and new work methods, experience is not necessarily an asset. Knowledge and proficiency in modern work techniques are a must. Here is where merit comes in."*

Example: 2: The topic is "Should States be given more autonomy?" Mr Vivek is speaking in favour. He is saying though there is the demarcation of subjects between the Union and States, but centre dictates states in the matter of financial aid, grants, posting of Administrative Service officers, appointment of Governors etc. These are against the spirit of the federal structure.

He keeps on speaking for a while. You can interrupt him by saying *"I am glad that Mr. Vivek has brought up this point. In fact, Sarkaria Commission has recommended that any politician should not be appointed in opposition-ruled states".*

Example: 3: The topic is "Should workers be included in management". Ameliya while speaking in favour says there is often a clash between them, yet; both want the prosperity of the organization. So, it's wise that workers are associated with management. Further...................

You may interrupt her by saying *"Very well said Ameliya. Workers have a sense of belongingness to the organization. Worker participation in many organizations has been successful. Time has come when workers should be included in management".*

Example: 4: Topic is "Should capital punishment be abolished". Harry is speaking against the abolition of capital punishment. You have to interrupt him to take your chance to speak.

You can interrupt him by saying "I agree with Harry. If a person guilty of the rarest of rare crimes is not awarded capital punishment, there will be no exemplary punishment to society".

Example: 5: The topic is "Should the state pass legislation for a complete ban on drugs inhaling used for high?" George says inhaling of drugs harms the person but the entire family and society. Notwithstanding............

You interrupt, "*Very correct. I would like to supplement what George has just said. It also affects children and next generation*".

Example: 6: Topic is "Is it right to enhance marriage age to 21". JACK is speaking of enhancing marriage age.

After a while you interrupt him, "*You have made a very important point. Let me elaborate it. Before 21 years a man is not emotionally and financially stable to support his family. Female too could not complete her studies to get a job by that age*".

5. Sentences **not to be used** to interrupt:

Never use the following sentences to interrupt:

That will never work.

That is crazy.

The idea is not a practical one.

You are wrong. How can that be?

You do not know what you are talking about.

That is ridiculous. What you are talking about?

Why you are so confused? We are talking about something else.

Examples of the wrong way to interrupt:

That is crazy! You do not know what you are talking about. You are trying to say that...

Do you think that liberalization has solved the problem? How that can be?

That will never work in this country.

To sum up, if think you are unjustly denied to speak, be assertive to say. However, wait for the right opportunity to interrupt and make interruptions skillfully to present your points.

6. How to look different:

Try to look different so that you are noticed and heard. While doing so, don't overdo or show over-enthusiasm. Follow these simple tips:

1. Try to lay down the scope of discussion by outlining the scope of discussion in the beginning, so that everyone talks on same thing.

2. Try to break down the topic in smaller fragments like cause, effect, etc. and discuss, one by one, throughout the discussion, so that your presence is felt throughout the discussion.

3. Try to present a fresh point when the group is struck at a particular point.

4. When there is chaos in the group, you must make an initiation to restore normalcy.

5. You should not speak for the sake of speaking, instead; you must make a positive contribution so everyone listens.

6. Initiate to bring consensus in the group. However, do not agree with others simply to make a consensus.

7. Concentrate on giving solutions instead of problems.

8. Try to resolve conflicts and arguments in the group. You must summarise the discussion at the end. This will show your team spirit.

7. How to Handle Awkward Situation?

Remember, there is opportunity in every difficulty. Try to locate and utilize that. Below are some awkward situations in GD and how to handle them.

Situation: 1: No idea about the topic:

Do not worry. Relax. All is not lost, as yet. A candidate is judged by several qualities, of which is one is knowledge of the topic. Listen to others. You will acquire some knowledge about the topic. Ask some questions. Supplement the topic by asking questions related to the topic. You should be seen as interested, understanding of the topic and contributing in the discussion. At last, you should try to summarise the discussion.

Situation: 2: Unanswerable Question:

If participants ask you a question, be sure you understand it. If you are not clear ask to explain the question by counter question. If you know the answer, reply it. When you do not know the answer, say you do not know and ask if anybody can focus on the issue.

Situation: 3: Side Conversation:

If two or more participants have formed a sub-group, having side conversations and not paying attention to you or listening to your talk what you should not do and do. Don't embarrass them by saying: "Hey! Listen". Instead, to get their attention, you may do either of the following:

Ask them a question or opinion. Say "May the entire group benefit from your views?" If still it fails, you may be harsher but politely and say "May we have one discussion at one time, please."

Situation: 4: Repetition:

If a participant repeats a point over and over again, you may interrupt by saying, "Yes! We heard you said that...."

Situation: 5: Irrelevant Discussion:

If a participant asks you an irrelevant question, do not say "How it is relevant?" If he asks more irrelevant questions, tell him gently "We should limit the discussion to the topic for GD" or "We should discuss the important points first."

Situation: 6: When someone refutes your points:

Do not react and be irritated. It's natural in GD. Everyone may not agree with your points and may have different views. You should supplement your statement with fresh input preferably with examples.

Situation: 7: When someone ridicules you:

Such persons are egocentric. Do not show your emotions. Appreciate his points. But, do not address him, instead address the group that while you respect others' views, you have a right to present your views to the group.

Situation: 8: When someone is interrupting you again and again:

Calm him by saying, *"Just a minute, I am about to finish." "I have just one more point to make." "Just a few seconds."*

After you finish, do not hesitate to ask that person to speak by saying *"Yes Mr. /Ms. ..., you are about to say something"*.

Chapter 11
Types of GD topics

Let's understand the different types of GD topics and how to prepare for each of them. Topics of GD can be either of the following types:

1. Factual.
2. Abstract.
3. Argumentative & Controversial topics.
4. Opinion Seeking Topics.
5. Current topics.
6. Case-based topics.

1. Factual Topics:

Such GD topics require basic familiarity with facts and information on static and dynamic segments of the environment. Typically, these are about socio-economic topics. These can be current, i.e., they may have been in the news lately, or could be unbound by time. Under this kind of group discussion, you require in-depth information about the topic. You should be able to support it with facts and figures and your information should be substantial. A factual topic for discussion gives a candidate a chance to prove that he is aware of and sensitive to his environment.

Examples of Factual GD Topics are Cold War, and State of the aged in the country.

2. Abstract GD Topics:

Under this type of GD Topic, the panellist gives a topic which is absolutely out of the box. Abstract topics are about intangible things or cases. These are some random GD topics. Such topics do not require facts or figures, but simply judge your imagination and how well you can associate it with your day-to-day life.

These topics test your lateral thinking and creativity and also to some extent your thinking ability. These GD topics are meant to test the candidate's creative skills and imaginativeness. Such topics can be interpreted in different ways by candidates. Students need to think outside of the box while discussion. In such GD topics, your comprehension skills and communication skills are put to the test. The key here is to try to link up what others are discussing with examples, or pointing out related points. These topics are not given often for discussion, but their possibility cannot be ruled out. It is strongly suggested you go through these GD topics and write down your thoughts on these and various other abstract topics.

Examples of Abstract GD Topics: A Teardrop on my guitar, where there's a will, there's a way, 26 Alphabets, Infinite Numbers, A Walk to Remember, A is an alphabet, Twinkle little star, The number, Six Billion and One Gold, Sky Green Earth White.

3. Argumentative or Controversial Topics:

These can be generic or specific GD topics which involve arguments and controversies around them. These are argumentative in nature. Such GD topics can lead to an argument. They are meant to generate controversy and at the same time, judge the analytical skills of the participant to see if he or she can think rationally without any bias and arrive at a harmonious conclusion.

Such topics are given by the panellists so that they can judge the maturity level of participants. The idea behind giving a topic like this is to see how much maturity the candidate is displaying by keeping his temper in check, and by rationally and logically arguing his point of view without getting personal and emotional. You're negotiating and convincing skills are at a test here.

Such GD topics are, as the name suggests very opinioned and hence the differences start brewing in the discussion. In GDs where these topics are given for discussion, the noise level is usually high, there may be tempers flying. Restrain from becoming too aggressive or strongly abiding by one opinion. It is better to take a diplomatic stance in case of sensitive issues. Give the discussion a wider angle. If, as a participant, you are not in favour of what the other candidate is saying, you should be smart enough to put across your point candidly without bashing the speaker.

Examples of Argumentative or Controversial GD topics: Emigration restriction should be lifted forever, Beauty Pageants are wrong, and Women are better managers.

4. Opinion Seeking Topics:

In such GD topics, candidates are asked to put across their opinions or points of view. Here, panellists look for presentation skills and also the ability to work in a team, meaning that your leadership skills are also judged.

Examples of Opinion Seeking GD Topics: The voting age for women should be lowered.

5. Current GD Topics:

These topics are based on current affairs and the latest events-nationally or internationally. Current GD topics are aimed at checking your general awareness. If you have been given a current topic, then probably you are being tested on how updated you are with current affairs.

Examples of Current GD Topics: Is social media an inevitable part of marketing? IT industry is going to create huge job opportunities in the country this year.

6. Case Study Topics:

Under a case-based study, a situation or a scenario is left to students for an open discussion. The information about the situation will be provided to you, a problem regarding the same situation will be given and all you will be asked for is to resolve it. These are open-ended discussions, wherein nobody is right or wrong, using their thinking ability they decide what they can do in such situations.

The case study tries to simulate a real-life situation. Information about the situation will be given to you and you would be asked as a group to resolve the situation. In the case study there are no incorrect answers or perfect solutions. The objective in the case study is to get you to think about the situation from various angles. The panelist under the case-based study, look for the decision-making skills, his or her ability to work in a team etc.

Examples of Case Study Topics are given in last chapter of this book.

Chapter 12

Skills for GD

In any kind of group discussion, the aim is to judge the participants based on personality, knowledge, communicative skills and leadership skills. Today team players are considered more important than individual contributors. The evaluators generally assess the competence of a candidate in terms of team listening, apt language, clarity of expression, positive speech attitudes, clear articulation and nonverbal communication.

In today's competitive age, communication skills are very important and essential. Subject knowledge is important but communication skills are as important as subject knowledge because without expression the knowledge is of no use.

In a group discussion, a candidate has to talk effectively so that he is able to convince others. Like any other oral communication, clear pronunciation, simple language, and right pitch are the

prerequisites of a group discussion.

A candidate who is successful in holding the attention of the audience creates a positive impact. Lack of active listening is often a reason for failure of communication.

By participating as an active listener, he/she may be able to contribute significantly to the group deliberations. Effective communication would also imply the use of correct grammar and vocabulary, and the use of simple and specific language. When there is clarity of thought, there is clarity in the use of language.

Along with in-depth knowledge, a positive attitude is an important element for participation in group discussions. Sometimes the panelist gives a particular topic to the candidate to test the candidate's positive or negative aspects of the candidate's attitude. One should stay confident and show interest in discussion, stay calm, and cheerful and take part energetically in group discussion. Hope and optimism are two

essential components of a positive attitude.

During the group discussion, keep it in mind that you are speaking not for yourself but for others to listen and respond. An individual must also learn the art of voice modulation. Try to keep your voice polite, and soft but convincing. One must also avoid the use of slang words.

One of the common misconceptions about leadership is that the leader is one who controls the group, but it is not true. In a group discussion, a participant with more knowledge, and more confidence; one who can find some solution to the problem and display initiative and responsibility will be identified as a leader.

A good leader makes sure that all the members of the team participate and when there is a problem, try to deal with it amicably. Leaders should know how to deal with the people who interrupt the GD. The leader in a group discussion should be able to manage the group despite differences of opinion and steer the discussion to a logical conclusion within the fixed time limit. A good leader also has decision-making and problem-solving ability. It means that a candidate must possess the ability to see through a difficult problem and find ways to reach a mutual agreement.

Analytical skills and objectivity are essential parts of GD where a candidate shows his ability to use his knowledge in its right context at the appropriate time or situation and this also shows that the candidate is capable of analysing the problem and solving it. With patience and the use of common sense, one can develop analytical skills. The problem-solving attitude can be seen when one uses skills in trying to reach a consensus.

When two or more people work towards achieving a goal, the feeling of cooperation can be seen. Actually, it can help in achieve their goal at a faster rate.

In a group discussion, this feeling of

cooperation may help in the following ways

(i) It creates a positive attitude among the group members.

(ii) If there is a cordial atmosphere, it will certainly help in reducing stress and tension.

(iii) It helps in increasing the self-confidence of each member.

Motivational Ability. This quality is required for all posts and it is one of the personality traits which is a must for any type of job. During the group discussion, the observers watch the candidates' ability to achieve his/her aim by getting the support and cooperation of other group members. A motivated individual can motivate the whole group and certainly find a solution to the problem.

Self-Confidence. Motivation leads to self-confidence also. While participating in a group discussion a candidate must have self-confidence, address the group as a whole and speak with conviction. Self-confidence is a quality which may help a candidate win the argument from other participants.

Use of Positive Body Language. During group discussion, a candidate must pay attention to his/her body language and posture. Verbal communication and nonverbal behaviour both play an important role in succeeding in a group discussion.

Suitable/ Appropriate Appearance. Our outfit or dressing reflects our external personality, group discussion is a formal gathering, and one must pay attention to what one wears. Casual clothes like jeans etc should be avoided.

Formal clothes like trousers and shirts for gents and sarees or trousers-shirts for females are suggested. Formal clothing certainly helps in enhancing one's personality as well as self-confidence.

Chapter 13
Mock GD-

TOPIC: Euthanasia: How Ethical is It?

(Each member is given a chest number for identity)

Scene at the Start of GD

All the members are of the same age group and have similar qualifications. The examiner explains the rules and announces the topic 'Euthanasia-How ethical is it? As the examiner withdraws from the scene, the candidates feel somewhat relaxed and a few of them resort to whispering aside, some of them remain silent and seem recollecting their thoughts, while some indulge in talking.

The noise grows louder, as some loud arguments between the candidates take place and others participate in settling the matter. We find No. 5 raising his voice so that he could be heard and addressing the group as a whole.

THE GD IN PROGRESS

No. 5. Please, please, my friends! May I request your kind attention for a few minutes? (*Tries to take initiative.*)

No. 2 I suppose No. 5, you want all of us to keep silent so that you could speak first. (Tries to cut the other down for self-gain, not a desired approach.)

No. 5 No, not at all my dear friend No. 2. I am not going to speak first on the topic unless all agree on that. I just wish to make a proposition for consideration of you all, so that the Group Discussion, for which we all are gathered here, could be started as per an order or sequence. Do you all agree?

(*Without taking anything personally, he clarifies his position and moves ahead.*)

No. 3. My dear No. 5, can you clarify the meaning of Euthanasia? If it means killing a patient, then how could it be ethical? Killing can't be treated as ethical.

No. 5 Yes, No. 3, euthanasia means mercy killing. It means mercy killing of those patients who are incurable and have been suffering for a long period but couldn't be cured and there is no chance of them getting cured. Killing such patients is ethical or not, is the topic of Group Discussion. Am I right?

(*Helping attitude, a good approach.*)

No.1 Yes, you are right, but it is very difficult to decide whether a disease in a patient is curable or incurable. The doctors of our country may find the disease in a patient incurable, but it could be cured in the USA. There is some hidden catch in this topic. It should be called suicide instead of euthanasia.

(*Suspicious and poor show of knowledge.*)

No. 7 Yes, it seems very strange to me also. How could killing a person be deemed as ethical?

(*Imitation and not a positive approach.*)

No. 8 What's strange in the topic? If No. 7 you are unable to understand it, better you withdraw. I don't find anything hidden in this topic; it is a very current topic. Recently, a patient asked permission from the Supreme Court for mercy killing, but he wasn't granted permission and after two days, he died.

(*Arrogant way of dealing with things.*)

No. 5 Well, friends, you all know that we have just 30 minutes to complete our Group Discussion. We have already lost 7 minutes, now we have only 23 minutes at our disposal.

(*Concerned to achieve the target.*)

No. 6 Yes, it's better that the Group Discussion be started without losing any time further. Let's hear No. 5, please.

No. 5 Thanks No. 6. I was saying that we should have two rounds and every member should get two minutes in the first round, and in the second round, one minute must be allotted to each of us. Let's start with No. 1 if he is ready to speak.

(*The candidate shows eagerness to get the task completed smoothly. He is not disturbed by sudden objections and clarifies his position well, does not lose calmness and tries to take everyone along. The candidate displays qualities of leadership and coordination.*)

No. 1 No, I shall not speak first. I shall speak in the last. No. 2 should speak now.

No. 2 Thanks No. 1, The topic of the Group Discussion is 'Euthanasia - How ethical is it?' It means that whosoever is sick, has no right to live in this world. Whether a patient is with an incurable disease is a difficult proposition to decide. Many times, it happens that doctors declare a patient's disease as incurable, but some miracle happens and the disease is cured. It also happens many times that doctors treat a patient for some other disease and the patient does not respond, but by chance, a small dose of a simple medicine cures his disease. Moreover 'life' and 'death' are not in the control of human beings. If we can't give anyone life, we have no right to take away life. So, in my opinion, euthanasia can't be treated as ethical. That's all.

(*The candidate shows patience and some originality of thought. He takes the responsibility assigned in good spirit. He can be groomed with training to suit the needs of the company.*)

No. 3. I don't believe in miracles as mentioned by No. 2 in his speech, but I agree with No. 2 that euthanasia can't be treated as ethical. How can we treat killing anybody as ethical? That's all.

(*Criticising others without any logic is not a good way to deal with the exercise.*)

No.4 I agree with No. 2. In my view, euthanasia or mercy killing is an unlawful act and an unlawful act can't be ethical. That's all. Thank you.

(*Lack of any ideas.*)

No. 5 Well friends, a lot of light is already thrown on the topic by No. 2. I like to mention further that the call for euthanasia surfaces in our society again and again, as it is doing now under the guise of death with dignity or assisted suicide. The patients with incurable diseases are crying out for help and love. Death can't be the answer to their suffering. Medical facilities, love and affection must be given to such patients. Suffering and pain is manageable these days. Withdrawing or withholding treatments, to let the patients die, is an unethical and immoral act. We must understand the difference between allowing nature to take its course and actively assisting death.

Both life and death, are not under the control of mankind. No human being has the right to take an innocent life, no matter how we try to justify it. God has not given us this authority. If euthanasia is treated as ethical for suffering patients, then where will it end?

Will the handicapped, or mentally retarded be the next? Then one day we shall also justify suicide.

The concept of euthanasia is in direct conflict with religion and ethics. If euthanasia be allowed and treated as ethical, it will finish all the moral, ethical and religious values.

So, in my opinion, euthanasia is not ethical either for the patient or for anybody else. That's all. Thank you for hearing me patiently.

(*Already has shown some important traits of his personality like leadership, co-ordination and keenness to achieve the desired goal. He knows how to present his views and has originality of thought and ideas. He has a balanced approach towards the problem. Deserving candidate.*)

No. 6 I have nothing new to say except that euthanasia is unethical and an immoral act, so it can't be regarded as ethical.

No. 7 I agree with No. 2 and No. 5. They both have spoken a lot about the topic. I have no more words to speak about the topic. Time is also very limited so I finish my speech.

No. 5 My dear friends, you know well, that the time is too short to complete the next round now. Only three minutes are left. No. 8, please complete your arguments. Please be kind enough to get this Group Discussion completed smoothly. We must not comment personally.

(*He tries his best to achieve the desired goal. Have respect and concern for others, and know how to tackle the problems in between.*)

No. 8 OK. No. 5, I would like to say that euthanasia is an unethical, immoral and unlawful act. I don't believe in any religion, so I am not quoting the word religion. Man must not be allowed to assist death. So, in my opinion, euthanasia can't be ethical.

(*His overall assessment comes to nil or negative.*)

No. 1 I like to thank you all for giving me a chance to sum up the Group Discussion. No. 2, No. 5 and others have spoken a lot about the demerits of euthanasia. I agree with all of them and have no more new arguments to speak on this topic. I endorse the views of No. 5. That's all. Thank you again.

(*Lack of confidence, lack of knowledge, suspicious.*)

Summary

Out of the eight candidates, Nos. 1, 3, 4, 6, 7 and 8 have not been found fit for the selection as they have a lack of confidence and no original ideas about the topic of the discussion. Nos. 7 and 8 have insulting and arrogant behaviour. Only Nos. 2 and 5 will be selected where No. 2 has original thinking but has to be trained to improve his attitude. No. 5 has emerged as the leader of the group, who took initiative and have a mature and helpful outlook, eagerness to achieve the goal.

TOPIC: Is Social Media Killing Our Book Reading Habit?

(Members are identified by numbers on the front of their dresses.)

Scene at the Start of GD

The examiner withdrew from the group after informing the participants about the rules to be followed in the GD and announcing the topic of the GD as 'Is Social Media Killing our Book Reading Habit?'. Soon participants start talking and whispering among themselves. Others prefer to remain silent and occupied in thought, noting their points on a paper. After some time, No. 3 raises his voice to be heard above the noise, addressing the whole group.

GD IN PROGRESS

No. 3. Friends, please give your kind attention for a few moments. We are discussing here 'Is Social Media Killing our Book Reading Habit?' and we have lost 7 valuable minutes. In the time left we must complete the discussion and reach a final conclusion. Do I have the concurrence of all to speak first?

(*No. 3 initiates the GD by displaying initiative and involvement. He is keen to conclude within the specified time, simultaneously taking the group along. He courteously takes other participants' permission to start, showing a cooperative attitude.*)

No. 8 No. 3, are you trying to bully us? You cannot start like that. Let us fix a sequential order of speaking in the initial round. Then we can have a rebuttal in the balance time to reach a conclusion. I propose that we go round in counter counterclockwise direction from 8 to 1. That way I will have to speak first, then No. 7 and so on. Is this acceptable to all?

(*Shows aggression in his first sentence, a negative trait. Shows initiative by proposing to speak first. The method suggested by him is the logical way to go about a GD.*)

No.1 Acceptable to me; I want some more time to jot down my points and prepare my speech.

(*Takes time to think, showing that he is a slow thinker.*)

No.4 Fine with me too. I think that is the best approach.

(*Supportive.*)

No. 8 Thanks, No. 1 and No. 4. I feel that social media is not affecting our book reading habits substantially, though being on social media eats up some of our time. By the way, how many people had a habit of reading books regularly before the advent of social media? Not school textbooks or help books, but other books like classical novels, religious books, fiction and non-fiction books. Not many, I'm sure.

Thus, I don't see the connection. Those of us who had a habit of reading books regularly earlier are continuing with this good habit. That's all from my side for the present. Your turn now, No. 7.

(*Shows excellent understanding of the topic with all its implications. Also, understand that social media takes up some of our time.*)

No. 7 Thanks, No. 8. I have strong feelings on the subject. Yes, true! Social media like FB, the internet, Gmail, etc. is killing book reading habits. People gather the information they need from sites like YouTube, Facebook, Twitter, WhatsApp etc., as these sites are created attractively and designed interactively. The people, especially schoolchildren, liking towards it increases heavily. All the latest news is fastly updated people so whatever they want to read or watch they prefer to do in these sites itself. This is the one strong reason people hate to read books. But book reading increases our knowledge in a perfect manner. Thus, these sites spoil the young future generation. That's all.

(*Uses ungrammatical language, showing his poor English. Also displays poor understanding of the subject, not knowing social media really means - Gmail is not social media!*)

No. 6 Thank you, No. 7. I agree with you 100 per cent! I have found this in my family too. Nothing more to say from my side, thank you.

(*Has no ideas of his own. Quoting a personal example should not be done. A poor thinker.*)

No.5 I agree with what No. 8 has said and do not support the thinking of No. 7 and No. 6. No, social media is not killing the habit of reading books. It is important for regular book readers to not only read books but also to explore different viewpoints on the subject being read.

Social media is the best way to do this. Using social media is also a logical shift due to the lower disposable time available with the fast speed of life currently. If one read books ten years ago, before the advent of social media, then one is likely to continue reading despite the presence of social media. I think social media and books are two sides of the same coin, but social media are better than books because times are changing, and with time we should also change

(She is supportive. Displays a good understanding of the topic, besides displaying that she has deeply analysed the topic. ,)

No.4 Nothing more to add to what No. 5 has said. I support her fully.

Thanks.

(Supportive, but has no ideas of his own. A poor thinker.)

No. 3 Thank you, No. 4. No, social media is not killing the book reading habit, as correctly mentioned by No. 8 and No. 5. In fact, it helps people to connect with others or to be social. With the help of social media, people share their knowledge and how know to improve.

Today socialisation is a priority; however, it doesn't mean that it is killing the book-reading habit.

Social media keeps us active and aware of day-to-day life. In fact, after we read a book, we can discuss it with people on social media to enable a better understanding of the book. Further, social media is helpful in discussions, connecting with people, having fun with friends remotely etc. But all these benefits wouldn't be much affected when one uses it in a limited manner.

Social networking kills creativity when people make it a way of life and hook on to it endlessly. Such people are not really book readers and never will be. That's all for the time being. Thank you.

(Shows his cooperative nature by taking the others along. His analysis of the topic is excellent, as he recounts the advantages of social media.)

No. 2 Sorry, but I don't go with the ideas of No. 5 and No. 8. Social media is impacting book reading adversely and the reasons are many. First, social media is an unproductive use of time, as it only entertains you and gives no food for thought. Second, the amount of education you get from it is much less compared to that from reading books. Most of the time spent on social media is spent in searching what others are doing or forwarding bits of information to others.

This time can be well spent in reading, which at least adds to your knowledge. Further, the use of ' new' abbreviations to express yourself on social media hampers your language development, which in turn affects your writing. Another important factor is the fast-changing content on social sites, due to which the attention span of the readers has been reduced. The important habit of thinking over some content and giving it time to percolate into your mind is no longer there. This is one of the benefits of the book.

Books cultivate the capacity to understand and think. In addition, good reading habits develop in us a better understanding of our experiences. On the other hand, social media mostly indulges the cravings of people more than what is good for them. Lastly, the role models who the teens follow are more active on social media.

Teens try to emulate them, sometimes creating problems in their personalities. That's all.

(Though he has a fair understanding of the topic, he shows flawed thinking when he says "gives no food for thought". He also mentions irrelevant points like that in his last sentence.)

No.1 As all my points have been covered by other participants, I will not add anything more except that I agree with what No. 2 has said completely. Thank you.

(Has no ideas of his own. A poor thinker.)

No. 3 As we have very little time left after the completion of the first round, I will, with the permission of all, sum up the discussion. We seem to be a house divided, with Nos. 1, 2, 6 and 7 feeling that book reading has been adversely affected by social media and the other participants not agreeing to it. In fact, both No. 8 and No. 5 have pointed out the advantages of social media over books. I also mentioned that people who interact endlessly on social media are not really book readers. Some points made by No. 2 merit comment. He first mentioned that social media gives us no food for thought. I'm afraid he has probably had a bad experience with social media. It is felt that social media gives us much food for thought. What No. 5 mentioned is relevant here, as he mentioned that with time, we should also change. Another important point brought out by No. 8

is the fact that not many of us are regular readers of books. Those who are, will not be adversely affected by social media. I think that sums up the discussion. Thank once again to you all.

(*Shows maturity, initiative and time awareness in summing up the discussion without being asked. He displays good teamwork by mentioning the contributions of most participants. However, he points out the flawed logic of No. 2 also, but very politely.*)

Summary

Out of the eight candidates Nos. 3, 5 and 8 will be selected as they have shown good knowledge of the subject. No. 3 has good analytical skills, he takes the other candidates along, which shows his team spirit and leadership. No. 5 displays her knowledge and analyses it properly. She is also well-read and supportive. No. 8 displays the quality of good knowledge with logical examples, but he needs to be groomed because of his aggressive behaviour showed in the start. Other candidates 1, 2, 4 and 6 cannot be selected as they show poor knowledge of subject. They have no ideas of their own. Even many a times they display many flaws and irrelevant examples to express their view regarding the topic.

TOPIC:: *Do Beauty and Brains Go Together?*

Eva: The topic of beauty or brain is interesting and requires a lot of brains to think over it. Beauty itself has a very wide scope, limiting it to just external appearance is not a wise choice. It's only the way one perceives it. For some, being intelligent is a beauty. How one talks, walks, behaves, thinks etc. all determines beauty. A brain with wise thoughts and intellect is considered beautiful. People who are kind and generous are beautiful. It's not necessary that everyone is born a genius but everyone can be beautiful just by mending some of its habits. Maybe that's the reason why humans tend to find beauty in everything be it nature, people or nonliving objects. Beauty provides peace and tranquillity to a person that's why a spiritually enlightened soul is considered beautiful. And not to forget GOD is beautiful, truth is beautiful, love is beautiful and all emotions that tend to make you live even for a day more is beautiful. As Keats said "Truth is beauty, beauty is truth. Ye all know on earth and all ye need to know".

Elijah: In my opinion beauty and brains go together because if you are smart, good-looking looking and you have a great personality but you don't have the good brain then there is no use of that. And the best part is as you all know that our beauty is in our heart and heart is connected with our brain. If we think positive automatically, we look smart. Because it shows our personality also.

Louie: Hello friends, I would like to say something different. As you know beauty comes from our heart and the heart works according to our mind means our brain. And you know very well if you think positively, speak well, and do good if you know how sweet to talk with respect, and where which work should be done it means your brain is working well and you are fit, smart and beautiful. All persons are attracted to you. And that's the way we can say brain and beauty can work together.

Dipika: In my point of view, if you have a smart brain then you can make your personality (beauty) very attractive and bold also. But if you have a good face or personality without having a good brain then it's like a day without sunshine means nothing. So, if you have a smart brain beauty will come automatically.

Saif: Beauty is not only physical. And I think the brain is the part of beauty (a mental beauty). So, if a person needs to succeed in life, he should more focus on improving his mental beauty rather than physical appearance. Physical appearance may help sometimes but beauty will help you get out of the trap and become a successful person.

Jake: First of all, I would like to know why it everyone is against beauty. I mean why can't beauty & brain stay together? There are so many examples of beauty with the brain. Didn't you know that many beautiful women took her career so well? Don't you guys think men are also beautiful? I mean we should not say about someone that looks at him or she is so intelligent and even so good-looking. We should see the two qualities differently. And for some beauty is the key to being successful and for some brain is the key to becoming successful. So, these two should be judged separately. The will to grow towards betterment matters hard work whether it's the field of beauty or brains.

Molly: According to me, beauty is not necessary for our life. If a person, of either gender with a powerful brain may achieve success in their life. Beauty is not a stable one, it may change by age, and only our brain remains constant. One can gain good respect only with his or her brain not by beauty. Only our brain can help us in our entire situation and not our beauty, with beauty you can gain nothing. So, brain and beauty don't go together.

TOPIC: *Do Women Make Good Managers?*

Louie: I think it would be justice with women if we say that they make better managers as they can do everything if given a chance to prove themselves. There are a number of ladies whom I admire having seen them working so hard and managing everything with so much ease. That possibly men can't even think of it.

Mukesh: Look at women holding positions at corporate, politics, and administration, who have managed the people so well we cannot deny the fact that women can be good managers. Moreover, what I believe is that nothing is impossible, if someone has the ability and if he or she works hard for it then he or she will surely achieve it. So, becoming a manager depends upon the qualities a person possesses and the hard work done by him or her but not on the gender of that person.

Duke: Hello friends, yes, I agree with the fact that women make good managers. However, it would be inappropriate to discriminate against talent based on gender. Anyone who possesses qualities like creativity, knowledge, commitment, versatility, discipline etc. can become good managers. But talking about the topic of our discussion I think women are way better than men in managing more stuffs at a time. You know back in ancient days men would go into the forest for hunt and the women used to do all the stuffs like taking care of kids, agriculture work, household chores etc. So, it shows that women are better at managing things from those days. Talking about the present scenario, there are many examples to prove that women make good managers. Thank you.

Mark: I would like to explain the word what actually manager means. A manager is a person who manages everything, take care the organizational profit, set up a link between his or her employee for further progress of company or organization. So, the definition reflects the post or the designation is not depending upon gender or sexuality. A Person having a good responsibility, personality, ethics, and capability of understanding the fact, leadership quality and communication skill can groom himself or herself for the post of the manager. There are plenty of examples where the managerial posts are hold by men and woman simultaneously. So, my point is that a deserving person should hold the right position beyond of any sort of sexual reservation.

Scarlett: I think managerial effectiveness does not rest on gender. It depends up on the ability, skill, and good knowledge of management. Both genders have same brain. Mind capacity depends up on hard work about these things. I agree now a day's women are good organizer and good manager.

Lucy: Well, the art of managing cannot be restricted by gender. Skills are to be learned and practiced. Men or women both can be expert with their opinions or judgments. But when it comes to framing any policy, designing a new framework, thinking of more economical means or managing a weird situation, I think men are better performer. I don't say women are better rather women should be given proper chance of letting out her views and trying her techniques of management. She may not perform better than men but she can perform equally well if given a chance. The better managers, men or women; we have, the better it is.

Toby: Dear friends in my opinion we are living in 21 centuries, so we cannot distinguish between men and woman, now women are managing job and home together. They are doing everything perfect in any field. Few years ago, people viewed work done by men cannot be done by women. But, now a days; it is vice versa. Women in many fields are giving their best. In conclusion; I would like to say managerial skills not depend on gender. One who has the ability who will be good manager?

David: Why do people stick on to the traditional beliefs that only men can become good managers? Those who possess the managerial talents, skills and ability to coordinate can become managers. It's not immaterial that only men can be the good managers. Nowadays women are also equally talented than that men in all aspects, so it's nothing that like only men can become good managers. Women take quicker decisions than men and obviously, they are successful in their work. So, I just want to conclude by saying that do not criticize women, as they can do anything and everything.

TOPIC: *Women are better at multi-tasking?*

Jessica: Women are better at multitasking. It doesn't depend on gender as far as multitasking is concerned. Even men can do all the work done by women, but the reason for women being better at multitasking is, in the past women had been managing their household work, but with the development and change in the society, they enhanced and participated in every field any achieve success.

Pratima: In my opinion, women have the situations and acquired the characteristics of a multitasking personality. Initially, they managed their home which required many different types of works to do. After some years, as men were doing the work in office women got some work outside the home. Furthermore, due to economic problems, women stood up for jobs also. Thus, women are mentally prepared for different tasks in life. Similarly, our culture and festivals are also held by women. They can manage home, office jobs and the social activities. They are maintaining different relationships better than men. All these things prove that women are better at multitasking. Now; there is no such a field where women are not working.

Alfie: According to my view, women are not better at multitasking. They do many tasks at home that are different but in any other job and management work they may not be good. In multitasking there is no difference between males and females. It depends on their interest and patience. There are also so many males good at multitasking. So, women are good but not better than men.

Joshu: Women are playing vital roles in our society. Women handle all types of problems viz., household problems, professional problems as well as political problems. They face all problems but do not mix them, it's their quality. Women always lead to solving problems. Women are better at multitasking.

Topic: Cricket *Has Spoiled Other Streams of Sports.*

Oliver: Hi friends, it is not proper to consider cricket as a national obsession. It is one game of which we are proud. Cricket has won the hearts of sports lovers. It has made it more popular than any other sport. Cricket is, and will be the most popular sport. I wish other sports also to do well.

George: Friends, I do agree with Oliver. I think alike that cricket hasn't harmed any sports. If cricket is very interesting, full of excitement, having a national patriotism feel, then it is not the sport's fault. I think it is just because cricket is a very interesting sport and that is why it has become so popular and loved by all. At the same time, I say that other sports have not lost their importance, whether it is tennis, badminton or hockey, they are still very popular. Yet; cricket is the most popular and followed by more people.

Harry: I don't think cricket as a national obsession is a deterrent to other sports. Cricket has gained popularity because of the contribution of cricket stalwarts. Due to the achievements of these people, it has become the most appreciated sport. So, if we want other games to be equally appreciated, then we need some great legends in other games too. I believe that if other sports will also produce great players, then definitely, they will get as much appreciation as cricket in this country.

Dinesh: Friends, cricket is detrimental to other sports, I agree with it. This game is promoted by different ways of advertisements. Cricket sports stars are seen in most of the advertisements related to sports items or promotion of other products. And the way it is advertised on the news make cricket not only detrimental to other sports but to national peace. In newspapers, most of the sports page is filled with cricket news, wherever it is held. As we all know media has the highest power today in our country, if they wish they can change the shape of sports too. To summarize along with cricket the media too is playing the role of detriment to other sports.

Rupa: Hi Everyone, I don't think that cricket is a detriment to other sports. It is our people in the country who have a supportive spirit towards cricket and this is what is destroying other sports. Most people do not even know that we have teams in Hockey, Rugby, Soccer, Basketball etc. I hope that we will recognize players of all sports as well as athletes of all games and support them.

Jack: Cricket is not at all detrimental to any other sports, it is suppressed by us. According to me, there cannot be a comparison between different sports. Each has its existence, so how can cricket suppress the other sports? It is just a matter of fact that people are crazy about cricket. So, the comparison lies not in sports but in our thinking only.

Jacob: Well, I feel that obsession with cricket is a detriment to other sports. It is all because of the way it is promoted. It is just like in the case of a movie, if a movie is hyped about, all of us go to watch it. But on the same time some epic movie just gets neglected because of poor advertisement. If other sports are unable to match up to the expectations, it is only because of improper training due to lack of finances.

Zenith: Well friends, I am a cricket fan & support cricket a lot but I too feel that it has come to a point where it has become detrimental to other sports. Check with ourselves, how many of us watch other sports. Of course, there are few but why so few? One strong reason could be the support & hype cricket gets through the media. People not only watch the match with sheer attention but also the pre- and post-match shows I would say that the government should definitely see to this and take necessary measures to allow other sports to perpetuate.

Rupa: To conclude the discussion, I would sum up the salient points of our discussion. First; most of us agree that the game of Cricket itself is not spoiling other streams of sports but it's the people of our country who go crazy for their favourite sport. Second; the media should give a similar level of exposure to other sports, as it does to cricket. Third; the government & other sponsors, who fund cricket, should do the same for other sports as well, so that sportspeople and athletes get trained and bring laurels for the country.

Topic: *We Will Never Be Corruption Free Society.*

Ameli: Good morning, everyone! I hope this discussion will be a very productive exercise. When it comes to predicting whether we will have a corruption-free society or not, I would say it is not impossible but also very difficult to achieve as I strongly believe that corruption is the price we pay for democracy. Corruption is the abuse of power and the people.

Charlie: Hello Friends! In a democracy, there is no room for corruption. Yes, there is rampant corruption in society, not only in the government services but also in the private sector. A lot of money has been looted. It is possible to have a corruption-free society. Think about it. A democratically elected government is answerable to the people, through the opposition party. Thus, politicians can also help in discarding corruption from the system.

Muhammad: Good Morning friends! It is very easy to say that corruption is unstoppable and to crack jokes about corruption. But; if none of us pay bribes to anyone to get the job done, it is possible to eliminate corruption. Government agencies might refuse to do your rightful job without you're a favor, but; if none of us do that, they will not be able to keep pending it after a point. This doesn't happen in a day, of course, but with a clear destination set in our minds, we can stop corruption. It needs a mass public agitation against corruption. What is needed is persistence and non-cooperation of the public. I also would like to mention that if corruption was the price paid for democracy, corruption exists in communist countries also.

Isabella: I believe it is possible to have a corruption free society in our country. We have many rights in our hands. If we know our rights and our responsibilities, we can surely throw away corruption from its roots. We have to change in the first place because removing corruption is neither a one-day job nor a man's job. We must stop giving bribes. We all must abide by rules and regulations then only the cure of corruption in society.

Isla: Friends! I believe that there is no room for corruption in our democracy. Corruption is the consequence of the unawareness of people. Corruption has to be stopped in any way and the main thing is to increase the awareness of common people towards this problem of bribes. The main power that could help in controlling this is the media. It could be the newspaper, TV or radio they have to start campaigns against this disease. They can contribute a lot in creating a corruption free society.

Ava: Corruption is the root of every evil thing that happens in the country. Nowadays, we see news full of corruption scandals by leaders of the country who are ruling the country. The common man has no options left to complete his work without giving bribes. Corruption will not end unless there is awareness among the people regarding the bad consequences on the economy of country for which a common man has to pay.

Rohan: Nowadays we can't find a place where there is no corruption. If we blame others, nothing will happen and even corrupt people won't change. So, we have to be mentally very strong and we must have the determination to make the nation the most powerful country in the world. That means not only in the sense of money, but we have to be respected by every person in the world due to our cultures and mindsets. If we dare to achieve a corruption free society, then we will be the number one in the entire world. We should have the confidence that we can achieve anything, not only a corruption-free society but also whatever we want to change in our society.

Topic: *Is Ethics in Business a Passing Fad*?

Oliva: Hello everyone! I am Oliva. I feel the topic of ethics in business is a fad is appropriate in today's scenario. Ethics and values are the soul of any business. If the organization can't resort to ethics, values and morals the business won't be a sustainable one. Truth always prevails.

Rishi: In my opinion, ethics in business is not a fad. To be in business and to retain in it, one has to practice business with ethics.

Cora: Hello friends, every business is run on business principles, practices and business ethics. Maximizing the profit is the sole basis of business. For companies, the customer and profit are more important to sustain in business. Social ethics is different from business ethics. In the good old times, businesses used to earn even less profit for social ethics. Today's scenario is different. Ethics in business is fading against the maximizing profit concept of business today.

Justin: No, ethics in business can never be a passing Fad. Ethics are the basics of a business. If a business wants to go long and earn more goodwill it will have to work on its ethics. Without ethics, if a business tries to earn more profit it will remain only for a short span of the time.

Rakesh: I strongly believe that ethics in a business corporation is not a fad. Any business which wants to be established with a huge esteem needs to follow its operations on the basis of ethics set by the policy framers. A business ' success and failure lie in the ethics which it holds. A company is known by its operations, products or services and ethics. All are important. So, the business will not dare to leave ethics.

Reshma: I firmly believe that ethics in business can never be a fad. Ethics are very important for the growth of business. Ethics relate to moral values. By using the wrong ways, a businessman can earn huge profits but only for a short period. Business is all about customer satisfaction that depends on truth and commitment. In this cutthroat competition of the business world, one cannot afford to lose valuable customers by not adhering to ethics.

Topic: Artificial Intelligence - Pros and Cons.

Audusa: Hi everyone; the topic for discussion is very interesting. Artificial Intelligence is a concept which refers to the programming which can make machines intelligent. In simpler terms, the program or machine is made in such a way that it keeps on learning with whatever output the machine creates. In my opinion, artificial intelligence is a boon to humanity as it can vastly create more opportunities for people.

Abeje: Hi everyone. As far as my opinion is concerned, the use of machine learning or artificial intelligence should be restricted and should not be made a way of life. It can have serious repercussions if machines become more intelligent than humans. In a limited environment, machines can prove beneficial but human intelligence should also remain in control on machines.

Virginia: Well, that holds for everything. There should be a balanced development. Improvements in artificial intelligence can create a world of opportunities. Consider the example of driverless cars which are being created by the leading tech companies in the world. With the sheer use of machines, AI-programmed software driving cars would become automated. If all cars were running on AI software, it could cause a reduction in traffic accidents, and speed control and there would be no human errors. People often get tired or lose concentration while driving. But with driverless cars, there would be no such situation. Hence there is a strong merit in artificial intelligence.

Pamela: Hi. In a few scenarios, it may seem a good option. But; is this not going to add to unemployment? Increasing machines and technological advancements have always created unemployment. If this is expanded across business sectors and is increased over the years, it could create a massive problem for the human race as there would be unemployment and hence more poverty, hunger and related issues.

Tushar: I agree with Pamela. All the jobs which humans do if done by machines would lead to mass unemployment and eventually destabilize the economic growth of countries. Further, it would limit the use of the brain in problem-solving and creativity in their work.

Navin: I differ from Tushar and Pamela. The advancements in artificial intelligence have not created unemployment but generated jobs which were earlier unheard and unknown. Various new opportunities have been created by using in artificial intelligence. In fact, a lot of new opportunities have also been created because of AI in businesses. Efficiencies have gone up, errors have reduced, timelines of deliveries have shortened, and all this was possible because of machine learning.

Gregory: Healthcare has vastly benefited from AI. There has been better forecasting, trend analysis, symptom reading etc. which has enabled doctors to make much by critical decisions within a curable period. Also, the use of machine learning in banking has enabled to reduction of fraud as irregularities can be caught urgently and bank staff can intervene on priority.

Raymond: There has to be a good balance between how and where to use artificial intelligence. Eventually, I feel that humans should have the final control over whatever machine learning or artificial intelligence program is being created. There can be no machine with artificial intelligence software that can substitute human thinking power and decision-making in different situations. Artificial intelligence cannot have human feelings, emotions and passion that a human possesses.

Case Studies Based GD Topics

In this method, the group members have to discuss the Case Study given Group Task.

The Sacking Dilemma Case.

You are the General Manager (HR) of a company engaged in manufacturing and selling costly cycles. Of late sales have drastically declined due to people opting for low powered gearless two-wheeler motor vehicle. The main departments are Production, Marketing, Accounting and R & D.

Prakash is an assistant in the Accounting Department. He has been with the company for 17 years. He is a competent employee discharging his job to the satisfaction of his seniors. But, of late; he is increasingly coming late for duty. He is married and has two daughters and one son. He says due to his family problems he becomes late for work. He always promises that he henceforth he will not come late. But never mends his way of reporting too late for work.

Sukumaran is the Production Supervisor. Since inception 35 years ago, he has been with the company. He has been very efficient supervisor. But age is catching up on him. But now young employees do not listen to him and undermine his authority making his supervision ineffective. If shown the way out, it will be difficult for him to get a job at this age. He is to retire from job in next two years.

Nitish, an MBA in marketing from a B-School joined the company two years back as a marketing executive. He has started advertising and marketing campaigns, at a heavy cost to the company. His plans made initial success but shortly sales came down to initial level. He handles company dealers in Eastern States. His initial success has gone deep to his heart. He feels disconnected when some ideas are not accepted by higher management.

Rakesh is a Marketing Executive with the company for the last 5 years. He is not an MBA, yet; was hired by the company due to his sharp acumen and practical approach. In the last few years, a good number of MBAs were inducted into the company. Because of them, he was denied promotion last year as he was a non-MBA. This caused bouts of depression in him, however; from which he recovered. He became very complacent in his work and at times very rude to customers.

In desperate cost-cutting measures, the company must reduce its manpower. These are possible four candidates for termination.

◈ **Group Task**: You, as a group discuss and decide how many you will sack, which ones and why?

SET: 27: *Willy & Willy Case.*

You are the Chief Manager (Sales & Material Management) in a multinational company Willy & Willy. It is an animal trading company. Your present responsibility is to get cats, rats and dogs from Asian countries and supply them at profit to Western countries as pets. Of these dogs are seasonal whose availability remains higher if three months following winter. These days, the price of pet dogs is much higher in Western countries. You are expected to make a huge profit to the company which in turn will make a swift advancement in your career.

In the middle of procurement season, the Audit Team disclosed that Mr Gorge, the star performer Procurement Manager had quietly siphoned $14,000 from a company that customers had paid. The Gorge has excellent relations with customers, as such; without him, it would be difficult to achieve the target. Gorge admitted that he had taken money as he was badly in need of meeting the medical bill of his wife undergoing treatment for a serious ailment. Following this finding, the Audit team also found irregularities in a few other departments. However; your department was the first one where irregularity was detected. The company is known for the integrity of its employees. This is the first time such a thing happened.

◇ **Task:** People are looking as what action you will take. State what would you do?

Tuna Tuna Case.

The Sea Sore Cooperative (SSC), Kolkata was established in 2015. Its prime business was to collect fish from fishermen and sell them for better returns to fishermen. SSC could produce only up to 7, 0000 cans per year because of manpower constrain. Yet; it had earned a net profit of Rs.15, 000. SSC stepped up production. It has an unsold inventory of 3,000 cans amounting to Rs. 8.000. Last year, a Private Limited Company named FISCO was established in Kolkata doing fisheries business. It focused on selling diversified fish in urban areas. FISCO canned Skipjack Tuna fish. Its meat was harder and different than yellowfin tuna. FISCO canned and marketed Yellow Fin Tuna at a lower price than the higher-priced Skipjack Tuna fish of SSC. Because of the higher overhead cost, its selling price was higher than yellowfin tuna. The demand for canned Tuna is only in upcountry areas. The management of SSC is pondering over what the problem was and how to resolve it from both short- and long-term perspectives.

◈ **Group Task**: How to resolve it in both short- and long-term perspectives?

Brown Melons Case

You are the Manager, in Qatar Qatar-based exotic fruits procuring and selling company, Bulls & Bulls. Brown Melons are cultivated in an oasis in the Sahara Desert. Worldwide sales of this product were almost constant at 200 melons a year. Traditionally; its customers were Arabian Sheikhs and celebrities of Hollywood and Bollywood. It is now proven that Brown Melons have medicinal value for some incurable fatal syndromes in women. The Brown Melon of Bulls and Bulls are badly demanded by a voluntary Swedish organization to treat poor African women. Patients in those countries cannot afford to pay the price of Brown Melons of Bulls & Bulls. You know revenues from treating patients will be much lower than selling to Sheiks and film celebrities.

◈ **Task**: State what would you do in the situation.

Secret Information Case.

Mr. George, the Corporate HR Head is a polite, nice, helping person liked by employees. Smith approaches him for a job saying he is jobless. Mr. George takes his resume and asks him to see him after fifteen days. Mr. Smith meets him after fifteen days. Mr George tells him to come after some time as he could not find a job for him. The meeting goes on. Mr. George develops a friendship with him.

One day Mr. Smith confides with him that for a crime he was sentenced to 15 years and has been in jail for the last eight years and has run out of jail and the police are looking for him. Mr George tells him to see him after two days and he will give him a job. However, as he leaves, Mr George calls the police and gets Mr. Smith arrested.

Because of this betrayal of trust, employees started losing trust in Mr. George. Someone reported this to the Executive Director to whom Mr. George reports.

◇ **Task:** Suppose you are that Executive Director. How would deal with the situation?

In a Fix Case!

You are a young blue-eyed dynamic boy in a reputed geyser marketing firm. Under your leadership, the firm has got an edge over other competing firms. You have top management convinced that the firm should enter into the filmmaking business.

You made a film division of the firm and hired Mr Venu, Mr Anu and Mr Kashyap in the film division. They are given full autonomy in their task. Initially, things went well. After three months Mr. Venue, with tears tells you he quiets the job. In the fifth month, Mr. Anu leaves on some pretext. The only left member Mr. Kashyap says that he can make a turnaround if given complete freedom. Meanwhile, the financial position of the company declined. You see your future as dark as you diverted the firm from marketing geysers in which it specializes.

◇ **Task**: State what you think went wrong and what should you do now.

Tension on the Job Case.

Sujit had been an exceptionally bright student at IIT Mumbai. He had few friends who liked him. He was liked by all his professors. Sujit joined TATA MOTORS from the campus as a production supervisor. Sujit supervised shop floor operations and in a shift 50 operators used to report to him.

The operators, by doing the same job for so many years, had developed a highly robotic style of functioning and were highly resistant to change. The trade union was powerful.

Shymal was an operator- in charge of the highly sensitive front axle assembly operation. Shymal, lately, had lost a lot of money in the stock market, had family problems and at times come drunk to duty. His abrasive behaviour had caused a shop floor problem. Shyamal also started absenting himself from duty and became casual in his approach. Subsequently, Shyamal was transferred to the quality control department to reduce his physical workload. Sujit could not find a suitable replacement for Shyamal in the assembly area. He had to frequently interchange workers who were unable to cope with the high-pressure work at the axle assembly. They deliberately started going slow, and thereby, affected productivity. Sujit did his best to solve the problem. He was under tremendous pressure from the top to increase productivity to previous levels.

The workers started demanding additional incentives and overtime payments. The management, on the other hand, was opposed to any change in the incentive structure. Sujit was helpless. He tried his best and at times did the work himself. The workers, sensing that Sujit had little control over them, became more aggressive and further slowed their work. Sujit suffered an emotional breakdown and had to stay away from work for two months.

◇ **Group Task:** Discuss the main issues in the case and what would be your approach in this situation.

Topic: Criterion- that you look for - in your potential employer.

You are fresh out of college and applying for jobs. You have received many interview calls. Rank the following criterion- that you look for - in your potential employer. Discuss on top three criteria.

The following are the criteria:

1. High salary.
2. Consistent and regular promotion.
3. Challenging Job.
4. Lean organizational structure.
5. Interpersonal Exposure.

6. HQ posting within five years.

7. Attractive performance bonus.

8. Annual Company vacation.

9. Normal (9 to 5) working hours.

10. Lots of travelling.

11. Mouthwatering perks.

12. Chance to make 'tax-free money'.

13. Regular performance appraisal.

14. On the job counseling,

15. Stiff target.

16. Target-based competition.

17. Stable and risk-free environment.

◈ **Group Task:** Discuss and conclude the common three criteria.

Topic: Toxic Effluents & Stringent Budget

About a plastic goods manufacturing company that wanted to go for new technology to reduce toxic effluents but had a stringent budget. Also, if not opted for it, the government might impose it forcefully after some time on the basis of public outcry. The current level of toxins released by the company were within legal limits but a report published recently showed that the legal levels set for the toxins were lagging and the regulation to reduce the level of toxins could come soon. Further, the company was not generating very high profits due to already ongoing expansion plans. The introduction of new technology could create a problem of over-budget for the company.

◈ **Task:** Discuss and suggest what action the company should take.

Topic: What made GM, and HR dissolve the committee?

A person is recruited by an electrical company at a high salary. He works hard and enthusiastically but slowly gets loaded with more and more work. So, after a year when it gets unbearable to manage social and personal life, he quits. GM tries but fails to stop him. GM then appoints a committee to look into the issue. But then suddenly GM dissolves it.

◇ Task: Discuss, what made GM, HR dissolve the committee before it started working. What are the flaws in the recruiting policy of HR, and what made the guy quit?

Topic: What should be done at Woodhead?

Woodhead Company manufactures shock absorbers for automobiles. It has two production managers, Samuel and Alexander. Alexander believes that workers are a priority. He believes in keeping his workers happy and provides every facility he can and never interferes with the work of supervisors. Though he was not able to provide the results and the plant was in loss under his management, there was no union under his management period. The Woodhead Company was taken over by the company, whose management replaced Alexander with Samuel. Samuel thinks the opposite of Alexander. He believes that he should take strict measures and that workers should not be given much importance. He used measures of firing workers if they didn't work properly. He did cost-cutting and many other things. During his time, the company did make a profit and even the cost of production was less. But all this led to anger among workers. Many supervisors left, and he was facing difficulty in recruiting new employees and there were talks about the creation of a union.

◇ **Task:** Finally; there were two questions: Who is an ideal manager? And what should be done in this situation? Discuss.

Topic: Charlie Bunking the Classes for The Course He Joined.

Charlie was working for a company for 7 years. He wanted a promotion. He joined a six-month training course offered by his company where a good performance would get him a promotion. He was a good student in school. So, he isolated himself for the first month of the course and he kept studying. On his first assessment exam, he got a grade of B. Other grades were A+, A, B+, and B (nothing was mentioned that A+ is the highest or B is lowest). The guy got depressed after his performance. His morale went down. He started bunking the classes for the course he joined. Discuss: What could be the possible reason for his performance? What kind of expectations he had from his current job?

◈ **Task:** What should the course coordinator do to boost the guy's morale?

Topic: They have plans to quit.

Zeco Ltd. Company workers are angry as their salary is less than that of employees hired later. They want HR to resolve the matter in a day. But HR neglects the scenario for two days. Then Operations manager intervenes and solves the matter. Workers start working more and have to sometimes work even at weekends. Then after some time, they start realizing that hopes of better remuneration are not realistic. So frustrated with the unknown workload they have plans to quit.

◈ **Task:** What should be done now?

Topic: Also, he has an ailing mother.

A young port engineer is proud to be the executor of a multi-million-dollar repair of one of the ships of his shipping company. But then he finds that the contracted firm has overcharged his company by 1/3rd of the original amount, which he then brings to his boss's notice. Though the officials then set up a meeting, they agree to split the amount and seem to him to be very cavalier about the entire deal. He then realizes that though the company respects his integrity, they will not do anything about this (i.e., they are corrupt themselves). If he does not sign the passing order, he may lose his job, and there were not many companies offering the kind of role he wanted. Also, he has an ailing mother.

Task: What can he do now?